Essays on
Historical
Materialism

Essays on
Historical
Materialism

Edited by
John Rees

BOOKMARKS

London, Chicago and Sydney

Essays on Historical Materialism – Edited by John Rees
First published 1998
Bookmarks Publications Ltd, c/o 1 Bloomsbury Street, London WC1B 3QE,
England
Bookmarks, PO Box 16085, Chicago Illinois 60616, USA
Bookmarks, PO Box A338, Sydney South, NSW 2000, Australia
Copyright © Bookmarks Publications Ltd

ISBN 1 898876 38 X

Printed by BPC Wheatons Ltd, Exeter
Cover by Sherborne Design

**Bookmarks Publications Ltd is linked to an international grouping of
socialist organisations:**
- **Australia:** International Socialist Organisation, PO Box A338, Sydney South
- **Britain:** Socialist Workers Party, PO Box 82, London E3
- **Canada:** International Socialists, PO Box 339, Station E, Toronto, Ontario
  M6H 4E3
- **Cyprus:** Ergatiki Demokratia, PO Box 7280, Nicosia
- **Czech Republic:** Socialisticka Solidarita, PO Box 42, Praha 42, 140 02
- **Denmark:** Internationale Socialister, Postboks 642, 2200 København N
- **Greece:** Socialistiko Ergatiko Komma, c/o Workers Solidarity, PO Box 8161,
  Athens 100 10
- **Holland:** Internationale Socialisten, PO Box 92025, 1090AA Amsterdam
- **Ireland:** Socialist Workers Party, PO Box 1648, Dublin 8
- **New Zealand:** Socialist Workers Organisation, PO Box 8851, Auckland
- **Norway:** Internasjonale Socialisterr, Postboks 5370, Majorstua, 0304 Oslo 3
- **Poland:** Solidarność Socjalistyczna, PO Box 12, 01-900 Warszawa 118
- **South Africa:** Socialist Workers Organisation, PO Box 18530, Hillbrow
  2038, Johannesburg
- **Spain:** Socialismo Internacional, Apartado 563, 08080, Barcelona
- **United States:** International Socialist Organization, PO Box 16085, Chicago,
  Illinois 60616
- **Zimbabwe:** International Socialist Organisation, PO Box 6758, Harare

Contents

Introduction

John Rees

Marxist ideas have enjoyed three major periods of renewal in the 20th century. The first and greatest came in the aftermath of the Russian Revolution and the revolutions it sparked in the rest of Europe, beginning in 1917 and running into the late 1920s. The second followed quickly, a product of the radicalisation which accompanied the rise of fascism in the 1930s and which also informed the wartime resistance movements in France, Italy and Greece. This second revival, however, largely took place under the aegis of Stalinism. The third renaissance marked a rejection of Stalinism. It was prepared by the emergence of the New Left in the early 1960s, but achieved its full impact with the international revolt of students and workers which began in 1968 and lasted into the mid-1970s. In Britain especially the resurgence of Marxist ideas had been most pronounced in historical studies, identified with figures such as Christopher Hill, Eric Hobsbawm, E P Thompson, Rodney Hilton and with some feminist historians.

What followed the defeat of the 1968 rebellion and its aftermath was a prolonged international offensive against the organised working class and on the gains made by women, blacks, gays and lesbians and national liberation movements in the 1960s and 1970s. Naturally, this was accompanied by an ideological counter-offensive. Marxism was inevitably a target.

By the 1980s, bolstered by the growing popularity of postmodernism, the right wing critique of Marxism was well established. Notions of class were said to be insupportable. The revisionist historians of the English and French revolutions were disinclined even to accept the term revolution as an accurate description of the events they studied. The Russian Revolution was so great an upheaval, and so comparatively recent, that the tack had to be different in this case—it was simply described as a tragedy never to be repeated. Women's studies flourished, but there was no longer any inherently radical charge attached to them. Margaret Thatcher and Madonna appeared as equally worthy feminist icons alongside revolutionaries and feminists like Alexandra Kollontai and Sylvia Pankhurst.

In the late 1980s and the 1990s, however, the tide began to turn. The fall of the Stalinist states after 1989 produced a brief right wing shout of exultation, but pro-market ideologies crashed with their beloved markets in the slump of the early 1990s. Reagan and Thatcher were long gone and Labourism, pronounced dead in the 1980s alongside the class which created it, returned triumphant across an extensive international front. The popular radical mood long pre-dated a revival of interest in left wing thought, but the latter arrived eventually. Perhaps its official inauguration can be dated from 1994 when prominent postmodernist Jacques Derrida declared in his *Specters of Marx* that we were all inheritors of Marx and that none of us could reckon without his legacy.

It seems an opportune moment, therefore, to restate the virtues of Marx's method, historical materialism, and to attempt to dismiss some of the misinformation about it which has swept around its feet in the last 30 years. This collection of essays deals with some of the key debates of that period: the impact of postmodernism and the real nature of the Marxist method are examined by Chris Harman and Alex Callinicos. Lindsey German looks at the fate of women's history. Mike Haynes looks at right wing interpretations of the Russian Revolution, while Brian Manning examines the role of labour in the English Revolution of the 17th century. Chris Bambery looks at Britain in the 19th century and Mark O'Brien analyses postmodernism's effect on the history of the same period. Sam Ashman looks at the strengths and weaknesses of the remarkable group of Marxists who composed the Communist Party Historians' Group. The collection concludes with John Rees's examination of the limitations of academic Marxism and the prospect of a renewal of the classical Marxist tradition.

All but two of these essays were originally given as papers at the History School organised by *International Socialism* in London in early 1998. Brian Manning and Mark O'Brien's articles were written separately.

CHAPTER 1

History, myth and Marxism

Chris Harman

People might think that socialists would be much better occupied being out on the streets agitating than discussing history. Of course we are out on the streets agitating. But for us the question of history is an incredibly important one. Why? There is a quote from George Orwell's *1984* which describes the thinking of the totalitarian state: 'He who controls the present controls the past. He who controls the past controls the future.' That is, if a ruling class can stop people understanding where society comes from, it can stop them understanding the development of society and so consolidate its power.

Historically, it is amazing the number of incidences in which the ruling classes have set out to stop people understanding the past. My favourite example is when the first all-China Empire was established in 221 BC. The Emperor decreed that all books referring to the old traditions should be burnt: 'There are some men of letters who do not model themselves on the present but study the past in order to criticise the present age. They confuse and excite the people... It is expedient that these be prohibited.' People daring to discuss the banned books 'should suffer execution, with public exposure of their corpses; those who use the past to criticise the present should be put to death together with their relatives.' Similar things have happened repeatedly since—and still happen today in many parts of the world.

When the Aztecs established their empire over the area of Mexico and Guatemala, in the 15th century, they set about burning all their old records, so that they could invent a tradition which would justify the rule of the Aztec Emperors. The Spanish conquistadores in the same area 100 years later proceeded very

9

much along the same lines. They destroyed all Aztec temples and monuments and as many as possible of the Aztec texts that they could in order to eradicate the memory of an Aztec civilisation.

More recently there was the burning of books by the Nazis. Then there was Stalin's rewriting of history, the falsifying of pictures, of cinema newsreel, the prohibition of any discussion, so that historic documents of any importance were kept locked up, right in the depths of the GPU's Lubianka headquarters. In Hungary, until ten years ago, any discussion whatsoever about the revolution of 1956 was banned. Even to raise the question was to risk losing your livelihood, harassment by the police, imprisonment and so on. Similarly, in Spain until 20 years ago, the banning of *Guernica* was a topic you could not raise, in print, in written work if you were a student, or in conversation. The myth that the town of Guernica had been burnt by the Basques had to prevail to wipe out the memory of the first ever aerial bombing.

For ruling classes then history is an important part of controlling people's ideas. The first historic records we have, from Ancient Egypt and from Ancient Sumar, are King Lists. The kings made the scribes draw up lists of their predecessors, usually going back to a mythical god, in order to perpetuate the idea that the kings were the embodiment of society. That approach remains the key to much mainstream history right through to the present. I am told it is a bit different in schools today, but when I went to school you started off by learning the names and dates of all of the English kings from Alfred the Great onwards. An awful lot of history books today are still written on the same basis: as this ruler came to power, he allegedly did this, that or the other, and then he was replaced by another ruler and another ruler.

A different conception of history to the King Lists approach begins to arise when a society faces a deep crisis, and people in that society have to try to come to terms with that crisis. That is why the two oldest works of history—Herodotus's history and Thucydides' account of the Peloponnesian wars—were written when Greek society was undergoing great transformations. Thucydides, for example, wrote at a time of enormous crisis. Athenian power had been broken and society torn apart by military defeat. He had to try to explain it and needed more than a list of kings to do that. He had to try to arrive at some scientific understanding of the past.

10

The rise of modern history was part of the Enlightenment, the process whereby a whole series of 18th century thinkers across Europe, most notably in France and Scotland, faced with a changing society, tried to come to some rational understanding of it. So there is Gibbon's *History of the Roman Empire* and Hume's *History of England* as well as the writings of Rousseau, Ferguson and Smith. The attempt at scientific history, like all the Enlightenment endeavours, came from thinkers who identified with the rise of a new class associated with a new form of organisation and production, the bourgeoisie. They tried to understand and explain how society could be reorganised in the interests of the bourgeoisie. But to do this meant cutting through the King Lists notion of history, to replace a list of facts not relating to each other by some overall pattern.

It is very fashionable today to attack the Enlightenment. But anyone who wants to transform society has to defend its scientific approach and try to build on it. Conservative thinkers have always understood this. They react in three ways. Some claim there is no history. It says in the Bible the poor are always with you; they say today that your genes are always with you. Thus the denial of history becomes reference to abstract biological impulses, so that nothing ever changes and society never undergoes any fundamental alteration whatsoever.

The second reaction is the old claim that there is no pattern to history whatsoever. It is very popular today. Everything is contingent, it is said, everything is accidental, where we are now is just the result of an accidental chain of events in the past, we cannot possibly understand it and we should not even try.

The third reaction is to say that any pattern to history is something we imposed purely by our own minds. History is seen as a series of myths. This then justifies historians producing their own myths. The myths typically produced in the 19th century were the myths of the glorious nation, the 1,000 year old Croat history or the 1,000 year old German history. Everything was just seen in terms of the growth of the nation, the nation as an ideal manifesting itself in history.

It is against this background that we have to understand Marx. The development of his ideas took place in the 1840s, when the Enlightenment was still something almost within living memory and the tradition was still alive. At the same time he was confronted with the beginning of the irrationalist rejection of understanding history. What Marx did was to see the limitations of the Enlightenment tradition, but to try to go beyond it to establish a really scientific understanding of history.

He moved on from the Enlightenment approach in two ways. Firstly, the Enlightenment had always assumed that history had stopped with the present. As Marx put it, 'For the bourgeoisie there has been history, but there is no more.' Once the bourgeoisie were in power, they no longer had any interest in understanding change—indeed they feared it.

Secondly Marx saw that past historians had understood history in terms of ideas, in terms of political institutions, in terms of the state, in terms of the rise and fall of civilisations in some cases. What they had never done was to understand history as being a product of the activity of ordinary human men and women. Marx insisted that if you really want to understand human history, you have to begin with the simple fact that human beings, unlike other animals, have no means of surviving or making their livelihood in the world except by labouring together, in cooperation with each other. To get a livelihood they have to have certain social relations with each other, and the degree to which they are successful in making a livelihood determines everything else they can do.

The root of all social development and all social change lies with where human beings are—how they make a livelihood and how they relate together in the process of making a livelihood. As he put it in the early pages of *The German Ideology*:

> The premises from which we begin are not arbitrary ones, not dogmas... They are the real individuals, their activity and the material conditions under which they live, both those which they find already existing and those produced by their activity... Its premises are men...in their actual, empirically perceptible process of development under definite conditions. As soon as this active life process is described history ceases to be a collection of dead facts as it is with the empiricists...or an imagined activity of imagined subjects as with the idealists.[1]

He said scientific history has to start out,

> ...from the material production of life itself, so as to comprehend the form of intercourse [ie the relations between people] connected with this and created by this mode of production as the

basis of all history and to show its action as state, to explain all the different theoretical products and forms of consciousness, religion, philosophy, ethics, etc, etc and to trace their origins and growth from this basis by which means the whole thing can be depicted in its totality (and therefore, too, the reciprocal action of the various sides on each other).[2]

The starting point had to be the material interaction of human beings across the world to make a livelihood. If you do not start with that, you do not understand anything else. This is the account Marx summarised brilliantly in the Preface to the *Critique of Political Economy*—an account which is usually attacked by enemies of Marxism and by some of its would-be friends for its use of the terms 'base' and 'superstructure'.

It was very common at one time to say Marx was mistaken when he wrote these things, he did not mean them, they are a bit crude. But the notion of the base and superstructure, and connected to that the relationship between the 'forces of production' and the 'relations of production', is absolutely central to Marx's whole approach. If you reject it you fall, despite yourself, into one of the conservative approaches to history.

What essentially did Marx argue? Firstly he argued that human beings develop through history greater and greater ability to provide themselves with a livelihood through labour. This is what he calls the 'forces of production'—human capacity to control the external world. Secondly he argued that such development of forces of production cannot occur without continually changing the relationships that human beings have with each other. As they develop new ways of making livelihoods, new relationships between individuals grow up. These relationships then determine all sorts of other relationships throughout society. This leads on to the famous base and superstructure distinction. He argues that at a certain point in history development of the forces of production depends upon a minority in society grabbing for itself all the surplus over and above what is necessary to keep the mass of society just about living. Given a low level of material production, if the surplus is divided equally among everyone, you get a minuscule improvement in the livelihood of the mass of the population. But if a privileged group concentrates the surplus in its hands, it can not only provide itself with immense privileges, it can also guarantee further developments of the forces of production. It can

13

for instance make sure that dams are built, that canals are dug, that resources are given to people to travel long distances to get rare products from distant societies. It can also store foodstuffs for the future, in case of a famine or a plague.

In this sense, by exploiting the mass of society, this privileged group can have a progressive function at a certain stage in history. Marx does not ever argue that classes arise accidentally. He argues that at a certain point in history, for the forces of production to develop, classes have to develop. And he argues that without the development of classes you would never have had the rise of civilisation, the development of towns, the development of art, of writing, of intellectual groups.

But he also argues that no sooner does a group emerge which controls the surplus than it establishes institutions to solidify its rule. These institutions are the superstructure. There is first of all a state—bodies of armed men at the beck and call of those who control the surplus. Then there are institutions which provide ideological justifications for it—hierarchies of priests who pump out mystical ideas designed to cement people to the existing ruling class. So Marx points out that at any point in society's history there are three factors interacting with each other. There is the development of the forces of production at the base— human beings getting together, learning new ways of controlling nature. Out of development of the forces of production new social relations are continually being thrown up between people. Finally, there is the superstructure erected by any ruling class to try to prevent further social change undermining its rule. But that means curtailing improved methods of production in so far as they lead to new social relations which undermine the old. There is a clash between the pressure of the superstructure above, to prevent the change in social relations, and the pressure of the production process below to create them

A historical example will show how this contradiction operates. We know that after 4000 BC enormous advances took place in the forces of production in the area that is now Iraq. There were the first use of metals, the digging of canals, the building of dams, the invention of writing. Enormous development took place, but part of the process of that development was the solidification of a ruling class based on the temples by about the year 3000 BC. Without it there would not have been the accumulation of a big enough surplus for metallurgy, the building of dams and canals, a social layer freed from work in the fields to study writing and reading. We also know that, once the ruling class solidified, it then reinforced its control over the mass of people. It set out to stop ideas and social groups arising that might question its rule. It established state and religious institutions which were as monolithic as it could make them. Finally we see something else from 3000 BC onwards. It is almost as if the clock of history slowed down. The forces of production developed at a much slower speed, there were fewer new inventions, less advance in the productivity of the land and food output, until society entered a great crisis, in about the years 2,300 or 2,200 BC.

That is, a certain level of development of production was required in the emergence of a ruling class. The ruling class bolstered its position with a superstructure, a hierarchy of officials, armed forces, police and priests. They sought to control every aspect of society, and that limited further development of production. There emerged a clash between the superstructure and advances in social production.

This is exactly Marx's model. It is very different to the caricature of Marxism that is often found and which came from Stalin's distortion of Marxism. According to the caricature the growth of forces of production automatically leads to the development of relations of production, and that automatically leads to the development of the superstructure. It had a simple justification in Stalin's time. 'Life is miserable', the Stalinists said in effect. 'If we build up industry, remove all democracy and egalitarianism, one day we'll have democratic socialism—in the meantime we must murder people or throw them in the Gulags.'

This is not at all the picture that Marx presented in *The German Ideology* and the Preface to the *Critique of Political Economy*. It is a mechanical distortion. He presented a dynamic picture. Changes in the forces of production continue to lead to low level changes in the relations of production. The superstructure tries to freeze the relations of production. There is a collision between the two. This is only resolved if a class struggle arises, and a new class emerges which smashes the superstructure and carries the forces of production forwards. There is nothing mechanical in this picture.

There is no notion in Marx that it is inevitable that the new ruling class breaks through. He says the alternatives are the victory of the new class or the mutual destruction of contending classes. Now, the term 'mutual destruction' may be slightly too

15

strong in some cases. In Ancient Sumar and Ancient Egypt, there was a great crisis without a new class emerging and the result was stagnation rather than complete collapse. But there are other cases of complete collapse—the Indus civilisation of ancient India, the Cretan and Mycenaean civilisations of Bronze Age Greece, the Teotihuacan and the Mayan civilisations in Mexico.

Marx's picture is never mechanical. Marx understood that in Europe in the 13th, 14th and 15th centuries new forms of production emerged, based around artisans, the beginnings of the putting out system, some exploitation of free labour and the growth of merchant capital. There were new relations of production which clashed with old relations of production and the old superstructure. The result in the 16th and 17th century was the Reformation, the Thirty Years War, the English Revolution and the Dutch Revolution. Marx also understood only too well that, in the case of Germany, the inability of a new class to assure leadership of society did not result in the automatic advance of society, but led to society going backwards for 150 to 200 years. No German of Marx's generation who lived with that legacy could possibly have seen history in any other way. The idea that Marx's approach was mechanical is imported into Marxism by people who either want to caricature Marxism or to use Marxism for a different purpose.

At the same time, however, let us be clear. To reject Marx's model is to reject any sense of unity to human history. It alone provides a picture of how human society develops, of why different societies develop in different circumstances. Human beings made a livelihood, had to relate differently to nature, had to relate differently to each other, and different forms of society emerged. It is only Marx's model that sees a unity through history, which has a common beginning—that is hairless animals with big brains, working together to try and make a livelihood for themselves. There is a unitary beginning and a unitary end, with the establishment of the world market and capitalism, with all sorts of different patterns in between. If you throw Marx's model out the window, what you end up with is a completely random view of history.

This does not mean that all non-Marxist history is useless. What it does mean is that the pattern non-Marxists impose on facts arises from common sense. Sometimes the common sense is well meant, for instance in Hugh Thomas's history of the

Spanish Civil War. It is a good account of the Spanish Civil War, but it is based upon the sort of liberal ideas that anyone who read *The Times* or *The Guardian* in the 1960s might have applied to Spain in the 1930s. But that common sense can also reflect some of the worst prejudices in society—as with his recent history of slavery. The alternative to mere reliance on common sense is to pick up some idea of a pattern from somewhere and then to impose it on history. The French historian Fernand Braudel produced some very useful work. But the pattern he imposed was basically the idea of recurrent long cycles in history, without providing any justification for doing so.

Genuine Marxists have always had an advantage over other historians, because Marxists can provide a pattern which is not estranged from the facts. For Marx, the empirical reality is a reality which arises out of people's efforts to get a livelihood, the social relations this encourages between them and the clashes that result between different classes. The picture has not been imposed on reality—it comes out of reality. That is why Marxists have often influenced other historians, and Marxism had an influence which grew with the upheavals in the world in the 1960s. In Britain or France in the 1960s and the early 1970s, historians who were Marxists, or to some degree influenced by the Marxist tradition, were very influential.

There has been in recent years a movement away from Marxism, and people who claim to come from the left have launched very traditional attacks upon Marxism. These are the 'postmodernists'. They usually started off claiming to be from the left, interested in what they called subordinate history, that is history from the point of view of oppressed groups—the sort of history you would not find in the King List version of history. But they now attack Marxism. Firstly they claim it tries to 'reduce' everything to economics and class! Typical is an article by Patrick Joyce in the journal *Social History*. He says we cannot deduce gender from material life and if we cannot explain gender in terms of material life then we cannot explain class in that way either. 'Class', Joyce writes, 'cannot be referred to an external social "referent" which is its foundation or cause.' That is, you belong to the class to which you think you belong. Or, as he puts it even more crudely, 'it is very difficult to conceive of a structure of social relationships, or a structure of any "social" variables (occupations, income etc) as lying objectively outside the agent or the observer'.[3]

17

Consider what it means to say that 'income does not lie objectively outside the agent or the observer'. It means that, if you see children starving in Africa on TV, it is not that they have no income—it is just that you think they have no income!

Secondly they insist that we only know anything through our own concepts, or through our language, and that language, as Joyce puts it, is a 'conventional and arbitrary structure of relations of difference, the eventual shape of which is produced by cultural and power relations'. Basically what he is saying is that there are no facts in history. There is only what people have said has happened. So, for example, we do not know whether people starved in the Biblical days—we only know that they said they starved. The fact that archaeologists might find piles of corpses does not seem to occur to such postmodernists. But even if they recognised there were such, they would insist that, when historians pull the evidence together, they just impose an arbitrary pattern on the evidence. Therefore any history is purely arbitrary history.

And the third thing they say is all history is myth, so any story is as good as any other. Drawn to a logical conclusion, the Book of Genesis is as good an account of the origins of humanity as Darwin's *Origin of Species*. Any myth is as good as any other. We know nothing of any external world. Everything is just created in our heads. From this they go on to claim that attempts to attain knowledge of history are merely, in Joyce's words, 'the operation of power', the attempt of one group to assert power over another group. Therefore any total history, any attempt to describe history as a total process of the development of humanity, is really a power game by those trying to subject everyone else to their rule. In other words Marxism is Stalinism.

Once you endorse the notion that history is myth, of course what matters is the good myth maker. The logical outcome is to present fictional, made up stories as history—which is what, for instance, Orlando Figes does in his highly publicised book on the Russian Revolution, as Mike Haynes has shown.[4]

Of course, not everyone who rejects Marxism is a postmodernist. Richard Evans has recently published a devastating destruction of some of the claims of the postmodernists. He takes them on on the question of the Holocaust. If everything is a myth, he argues, why cannot the Holocaust revisionists be right? If we do not know anything, if there is no factual basis underlying any language or any argument we put forward, why should not the

Holocaust denial history be as good as any other history? Yet, he insists:

> There is a massive, carefully empirical literature on the Nazi extermination of the Jews. Clearly, to regard it as fictional, unreal, or no nearer to historical reality than the work of the 'revisionists' who deny that Auschwitz ever happened at all, is simply wrong. Here is an issue where the evidence really counts, and can be used to establish the essential facts. Auschwitz was not a discourse. It trivialises mass murder to see it as a text... And if this is true of Auschwitz, then it must be true at least to some degree of other past happenings, events, institutions, people as well.[5]

He is absolutely right. The example of the Holocaust falsifies the whole approach of postmodernism. A historical method which cannot deal with one of the most important events of the 20th century is a method which must be rejected.

However, Evans does not go as far as that. He ejects postmodernism through the front door only to allow it in the back. This is because he also rejects the Marxist notion of unitary history. This is shown especially in his treatment of two very fashionable books—Schama's on the French Revolution and Figes' on the Russian Revolution. Evans says they are 'brilliantly written narratives'. Yet he admits they both rely on 'detailed sub-plots and biographies whose selection is self-confessedly personal and arbitrary', and that they ignore absolutely central phenomena like the mass hunger during the period of the French Revolution. In other words, Evans reverts to the postmodernist notion that, providing they are good myth makers, historians can trample over the facts. And, of course, what counts as a 'good' myth is one that fits in with the prejudices of the time in which it is written. History then becomes a matter of apologetics—a genuine 'power game' on behalf of the status quo. People like Evans do not like the extremes of postmodernism, but they reject the Marxist notion of a unity to history, flowing from the forces of production, the relations of production, base and superstructure, their interaction and the dynamic clash between them and the role of class in in it all. And so there is a drift back to the postmodernist ideas.

Finally where does postmodernism come from? It has material roots of its own. I remember the television series, *The History Man*, which was on the TV about ten or 15 years ago. It showed

19

a radical lecturer at a university, who makes his career by every dirty deed, and then ends up as a right wing professor. Post-modernism fits those sort of people perfectly. They played with Marxism in their youth, played with radical ideas, and now they have established themselves they end up putting forward ideas that are absolutely safe and tame and, in some cases, they are well rewarded for doing so. Rejecting a unitary view of the world, they can deal quite safely with odd quirks in history, in a folkloric way which nobody has developed before, without offering any challenge to those who dominate in the universities or in society

But postmodernism also has a second root, in intellectual history. That lies, in part, in what passed as Marxism in the universities in Britain, France and Germany, in the 1960s and 1970s. People still saw Stalinism as a valid variant of Marxism, and much of the left intelligentsia were half attracted and half repelled by it. In the case of E P Thompson it was absolutely clear. His intellectual upbringing was under Stalinism in the Communist Party. In 1956 he had broken from Stalinism at a practical level, supported the Hungarian Revolution and so on. But when he broke from Stalinism he believed that Stalinism was a version of Marxism, and therefore it was half a break with Marxism as well. He used to make a great play of joking about 'hysterical and diabolical' materialism. He would refer to himself as a Marxisant, not a Marxist. And, in particular, he would attack the base and superstructure distinction as a 'crude metaphor'. I do not think he ever understood it. That is why he attacked it as being crude. Unfortunately, his half break with Marxism opened the door for the postmodernists—although he would have been well to the fore in condemning them.

In Althusser's case it was even clearer. His first book, *Pour Marx*, translated into English *For Marx*—I prefer the English pun on the French title—can state, 'Stalin said this', 'Stalin was not completely wrong on that', as if Stalin was a serious reference for somebody who was an intellectual in the late 20th century. In reality Althusser started by taking for granted all sorts of assumptions from Stalinism and then tried to develop a theory on the basis of them. It meant that, effectively, he could not come to terms with the base and superstructure distinction and went as far as to develop an idea which Marx attacks categorically in *Capital*. Althusser said the base and superstructure distinction fits alright under capitalism, but in other societies the economy is not fundamentally determining. In some societies politics is the determinant, in some religion, in some other aspects. What is amazing is that in *Capital* Marx takes on precisely this argument in dealing with the claim that mode of production was determining under capitalism but not in the Middle Ages where religion dominated, or in ancient Rome and Athens where politics was supreme: 'This much is clear. The Middle Ages could not live on its Catholicism nor the ancient world on politics. On the contrary, it is the mode in which they gained a livelihood which explains why here Catholicism and there politics played a chief part.'

Althusser's whole structure was based upon the break with Marxism, and became ever more complicated and scholastic. He first claimed that economics determined the last instance, then the 'last instance never comes', then economics is not the determining factor, it is a 'structurally determining' factor. He moved increasingly away from Marx's unitary account of human history and denounced those who tried to defend that approach for 'historicism' and 'humanism'. What is more, on the fundamental question of the forces and relations of production, he turns Marx on his head. Marx argued that the forces of production continually give rise to new relations of production which begin to tear society apart. The metaphor Marx uses is of the kernel of the new society growing until it clashes with the integument (ie shell) of the old society, breaking it apart. By contrast Althusser said that the relations of production are determinant, not the forces of production. And I think we can explain that. For Stalin, the forces of production had to completely determine mechanically the relations of production as a justification for the horrors of state capitalist industrialisation. But by the 1970s Althusser identified with Mao in China, and, faced with China's economic backwardness, the Maoists concluded at the time of the 'Cultural Revolution' that they could only advance the forces of production by voluntarism, by massive changes in the relations of production. In effect, they said, 'Wave the Red Book and don't worry about eating.' Althusser gave an intellectual expression to this mood.

Althusserianism, like Maoism, is now a dead force. But such ideas still prevail, even among people who ostensibly reject them, like the so called 'political Marxists' Bob Brenner and Ellen Meiksins Wood. If you read their works, you will find little about how people get a livelihood from nature So the material forces of production hardly appear either in Brenner's writings on feudalism or in Wood's book on Greece. I think this is a reflection of the life of certain academics who live 1,000 miles from the real world. And nothing suits them better than the idea that intellectual thought proceeds by itself, that all that matters is changing intellectual ideas, change in relations, not the forces of production on the ground.

One additional point has to be made about the 'Marxism' of the 1960s and 1970s. It rejected Engels' account of primitive Communism, the rise of class society and the oppression of women. The Althusserians took it for granted that women had always been oppressed and that there had always been hierarchy. It is amazing that they did so, just as certain mainstream archaeologists and anthropologists were beginning to develop theories of evolution in society and to refer to Marx and Engels as serious references that people could learn from. But once the would-be Marxists had thrown Engels out the window, they had to see the oppression of women as having completely different roots to those of class. The next logical step was to denounce Marxism as 'reductionist' and 'essentialist' for seeing some pattern to human history. The Althusserians who were soft on Stalinism eventually ended up as the postmodernists who were hard against Marxism.

The polemics between Thompson and the Althusserians dominated much of academic Marxism in the late 1970s. Yet both sides in the debate accepted the Stalinist caricature of Marxism as a version of the real thing. This explains how disciples of both are now to be found in the vanguard of postmodernism.

The end result is a view of history which simply reiterates the 19th century conservative reaction to the Enlightenment. But it can only do so by ignoring or distorting a mass of empirical evidence—which is why it is so scathing in its denunciation of the search for truth. Yet in areas of study which the postmodernists do not dominate there is a growing pile of evidence that fits the Marxist account. For the study of ancient societies in the Americas, of Egypt and of Sumar, you find more of an awareness of the development of the forces of production, of how human control over nature gives rise to the cooperation between people, of the clash of state structures, of how society is thrown into crisis. In the study of the medieval period, while ex-Marxists and would-be Marxists are saying all that matters is the relations of production, empirical historians and archaeologists have emphasised the speed of the development of the forces of production in the 11th to 13th centuries, and again in the 16th century—an essential prerequisite for understanding the rise of capitalism. Again studies in the last 20 or 30 years show how the growth in productive forces in Ancient and Medieval China again and again clashed with existing relations of production and led to great social crises. There is a great mass of empirical evidence of which only Marx's classic formulations can make sense.

All this matters, because a Marxist approach allows us to see where the present came from, and that the present is not unchanging. It allows us to see that history has not stopped—that the dynamic of history that we saw in the past is still present and still working itself out. Once we grasp that, we can see that any idea that class has disappeared, or that the class struggle will not be a factor in the 21st century, is nonsense.

Finally, it allows us to see that humanity has a unitary history. There is not a history for men and a history for women, a history for the rich and a history for the poor, a history for whites and a history for blacks, a history for straights and a history for gays. All of them come out of the same root—in the material process shaping social change and class struggles. Understanding that is the key to freeing the world from all forms of oppression and exploitation.

CHAPTER 2

Marxism and the crisis in social history

Alex Callinicos

The nature of historical inquiry has become in recent years an intellectual battlefield. The, rather belated, impact of postmodernism on historians has radically put in question our ability to attain knowledge of the past. To gain some appreciation of the issues involved it may be helpful to place these debates in a larger historical context.[1] During the half century between the 1920s and the 1970s, we can see the rise of social history. The liberal historian G M Trevelyan famously defined social history as 'the history of a people with the politics left out'.[2] This is an accurate description in the sense that much social history sought to place the kind of narrative of political events that had been the concern of conventional historiography in the larger context of the development and transformation of more fundamental social and economic structures.

This social history was by no means necessarily Marxist. The Christian socialist R H Tawney pioneered the social interpretation of the English Revolution. In France the secular republican Georges Lefebvre did the same for the French Revolution, while the school which developed around the journal *Annales* was notoriously contemptuous of 'the history of events' (*histoire événementielle*), preferring instead to study what Fernard Braudel called *la longue durée*—the long term geographical, economic, and social structures underpinning such superficial phenomena as wars and reigns.

Nevertheless the emergence of these various kinds of social history provided a relatively favourable intellectual environment for the development of specifically Marxist historical interpretations.

25

Thus Albert Soboul, Georges Rudé, and Daniel Guérin built in different ways on Lefebvre's studies of the French Revolution. In Britain, the Communist Party Historians' Group pioneered the development of 'history from below' and provided a crucial stimulus for the foundation in 1952 of the journal *Past and Present*, the premier English language journal of social history.[3] This version of social history put politics back in, but not in the form of the 'high' politics of dynasties and courts, ministries and parliaments: historians like Edward Thompson and Christopher Hill sought to rewrite history from the standpoint of the oppressed and exploited, the marginalised and the excluded.

The political radicalisation of the 1960s and early 1970s reinforced this trend. One aspect of the renaissance of Marxism produced by the upturn in mass struggles was the expansion of Marxist history writing. The foundation of *History Workshop Journal* reflected the commitment of a generation of scholars emerging from the movements of the 1960s to the idea of history from below. There were counterparts elsewhere in the world. As a result of the struggles of the 1960s, reports Peter Novick, 'there appeared something hitherto unknown in the American historical profession: substantial and systematically "oppositional" historiographical tendencies'.[4] Meanwhile in India, the influential journal *Subaltern Studies* was set up in 1982 specifically to challenge the top down view of the anti-colonial struggle put forward by both nationalist and Communist historians: a visit by Edward Thompson to India in 1976-77 had a seminal influence on a generation of Indian radical historians.[5]

The revisionist challenge

Since the mid-1970s there has been an increasingly powerful reaction to this trend. Initially this reaction came from conventional bourgeois historians. It can be traced back to the famous 'gentry debate' of the 1950s—the challenge to the social interpretation of English Revolution mounted by conservative historians such as Hugh Trevor-Roper and J H Hexter. But Trevor-Roper, while challenging Tawney's claim that 16th and early 17th century England had seen the rise of an increasingly capitalist gentry, did not deny that the revolution had a social interpretation—he argued rather that it lay in the *decline* of the lesser gentry. More recently, however, revisionist historians such as Conrad Russell have denied that the English Revolution was about either religion or capitalism, treating it instead as the unexpected outcome of faction fights among local notables.[6]

As the attack on social history has gathered strength, it has become more explicitly political. Thus the Tory historian Jonathan Clark justified his attack on what he called 'the historiography of the 1960s'—which he identified particularly with Christopher Hill—by appealing to 'the change of mood in the late 1970s': in other words, the onset of Thatcherism demanded that history be rewritten.[7] In France during the late 1970s, when a group of ex-Maoist intellectuals were leading an assault on Marxism, claiming that it led ineluctably to the Stalinist gulags, François Furet launched a polemic against the social interpretation of the French Revolution. In one essay, he announced, 'La révolution française est terminée'—'the French Revolution is over'.[8] The implication is plain: the revolution is over, and let's not have any more of them.

The thrust of this kind of revisionism as far as the writing of history is concerned has been essentially to reinstate traditional narrative historiography. The 17th century historian Mark Kishlansky, the author of a particularly odious attack on Christopher Hill, is a case in point. Keith Thomas, himself one of the most outstanding post-war social historians, describes Kishlansky's volume in the new *Penguin History of Britain* as an example of the 'prevailing philosophy' in 17th century political history of 'one damn thing after another': 'Social, economic, cultural and intellectual developments are all excluded... Instead the book offers an unbroken political narrative which largely eschews interpretation or explanatory generalisation'.[9]

Such work is, in the strictest sense, reactionary, rejecting the methods of social history, Marxist or non-Marxist, to return to describing the political manoeuvres at the top of society. A more recent trend, however, has been for the specifically Marxist interpretation of history to come under attack on a basis which purports to be more radical, certainly intellectually, and sometimes politically, than Marxism. Predictably, the biggest fireworks have come over the two great revolutions. The fashionable mid-Atlantic historian Simon Schama marked the bicentenary of the French Revolution in 1989 with *Citizens*, a crude but well written anti-Jacobin history which built on contemporary work on the iconography of the revolution, analysing the various ways in which it represented itself. Then came in 1996 Orlando Figes's   27

A People's Tragedy, an anti-Bolshevik history of the Russian Revolution written from below, in which Stalinism becomes a consequence of the primitive communism and tendencies towards irrational violence of the Russian masses.

Both these vastly overpraised books are more likely to impress the less one knows about the French and Russian revolutions. They were essentially media events reflecting an ideological climate in which, with the collapse of the Stalinist regimes and the entrenchment of a neo-liberal consensus among Western elites, Marxism has come under increasingly powerful intellectual pressure. More influential among professional historians has been the impact of postmodernism.

Postmodernism in history

This shift is sometimes called the 'linguistic turn', a slogan coined by the philosopher Richard Rorty, one of the main propagandists for postmodernism in the English speaking world. Historians have indeed become increasingly preoccupied with language, symbols, representations, and culture. Now, on the face of it, there is no reason why one cannot study these phenomena from within a Marxist framework. Indeed, there are a number of pioneering Marxist works on the subject. Much of Hill's writing, for example, has been concerned precisely with the examination of specific ideological themes and representations in early modern England.

The belief has nevertheless become increasingly entrenched that one can only study language and representations from within a postmodernist framework. One can identify three reasons for this. First, historians (in many ways a rather parochial bunch) are only just beginning to catch up with the more general infatuation withpostmodernism that became a feature of the ideological climate in the West during the 1980s. This has been reinforced, secondly, by a preoccupation with the nature of historical narrative which reflects the impact of intellectual historians such as Hayden White (himself a convert to postmodernism). Thirdly, the retreat from Marxism by some of the historians who earlier identified with it has created an intellectual vacuum in which it seems as if postmodernism is the only way to pursue historical inquiry from a radical perspective.

This third reason can be illustrated by the case of Patrick Joyce.

A social historian of 19th century Britain, he wrote in 1980 a relatively conventional Marxist text, *Work, Society, and Politics: The Culture of the Factory in Later Victorian Britain*. More recently Joyce has moved towards an increasingly strong commitment to postmodernism. Thus he wrote in 1991, 'The major advance of "postmodernism" needs to be registered by historians: namely that the events, structures and processes of the past are indistinguishable from the forms of documentary representation, the conceptual and political appropriations, and the historical discourses that construct them'.[10] This reads like a startlingly literal reading of Jacques Derrida's famous pronouncement, 'There is no outside-text' ('Il n'y a pas de hors-texte'), or, as is it more usually translated, 'There is nothing outside the text'.[11]

Joyce seems to be committing himself here to what Rorty calls textualism, a form of idealism in which, instead of texts being about a world that exists largely independently of them, the world itself becomes a text. Concretely this means that class exploitation and oppression of women are texts, not social realities. So Joyce writes:

> If gender cannot be derived from an external referent, then the same follows for class. It cannot be referred to an external "social" referent which its foundation or cause. This referent, the "social", is itself a "discursive" product of history.[12]

Class is thus in the head, or in the mouth.

Rather than repeat general criticisms of postmodernism which I have developed at length elsewhere, let me make just one critical point here.[13] Joyce's textualism implies that it is possible to reconstruct historical processes entirely in terms of their textual representations without invoking 'an external referent'—without, in other words, comparing these representations with what the historian thinks actually happened. These representations in turn can be understood without setting them in a context that goes beyond discourse.[14]

Now this position cannot coherently be sustained. Thus, in his best known book, *Visions of the People*, Joyce challenges accounts of the Victorian working class which trace the growth of class consciousness. He argues that the late 19th century saw instead the entrenchment of various forms of populism, that is, 'a set of discourses and identities which are extra-economic in character, and inclusive and univeralising in their social remit in contrast to the exclusive categories of class.' It was the ability of Liberal politicians such as Gladstone to address workers in populist terms, counterposing 'the masses' to 'the classes', which explains the strength of Lib-Labism right into the 20th century.

Joyce links this argument to the rejection of class as an explanatory concept:

> This is a book chiefly about social identities and about discourses concerning the social order… Interests are not somehow given in the economic condition of workers, but are constructed through the agency of identities. Indeed, such identities are as real as any 'interests' ever were. The formation of social identities is not therefore something peripheral to a broader social and cultural history, but is quite central to it. And this formation was something accomplished in and by language.[15]

Yet in the detailed analyses that follow, Joyce continually invokes economic conditions. Thus, discussing the development of dialect literature in the north of England, he discusses various factors before continuing:

> The reasons go deeper, however, and it seems necessary to turn to the particular blend of change and continuity in the economic and social structure of Lancashire, Yorkshire and the north east. Dialect was *made necessary by* the degree of change undergone, yet it was made possible by the powerful continuities of structure and memory that obtained.[16]

'Made necessary by…': this is a pretty materialist way of putting it. Joyce goes on to relate the emergence of dialect literature to the particular combinations of mechanised factory production and craft-based forms of work organisation that prevailed in the region, along with associated patterns of urban settlement and family structures. Summarising this interpretation in his conclusion Joyce reiterates that 'the processes of dialect production were related to Lancashire's passage to a new industrial order'.[17] This is just one example of how in practice he constantly slides between textualism and materialism, thereby subverting his official denial that there is nothing outside the text. This reflects the simple fact that it is impossible to sustain historical enquiry unless discursive representations are set within a largely non-discursive context.[18]

Marxism and history

Establishing that even postmodernists are forced to presuppose something outside the text does not get us that far. Ludwig Wittgenstein once wrote, 'I am sitting with a philosopher in the garden; he says again and again, "I know that that's a tree," pointing to a tree that is near us. Someone else arrives and hears this, and I tell him, "This fellow isn't insane. We are only doing philosophy" '.[19] Philosophers often spend their time proving the obvious. Granted that history is more than its textual representation, what positive reasons are there for thinking that Marxism offers the best approach to understanding it?

One of the distinctive features of Marxism as an approach to history is that it combines an understanding of Braudel's *longue durée*—of epochal transformations arising from long term tendencies—with the capacity to grasp the most specific and localised of struggles. Both aspects are present in Marxist historical writing. On the one hand, we have great macro-studies such as Geoffrey de Ste Croix's *The Class Struggle in the Ancient Greek World*, which spans more than 1,000 years, Robin Blackburn's uncompleted history of the rise and fall of modern slavery, and Eric Hobsbawm's trilogy on the 'long 19th century' (*The Age of Revolution, The Age of Capital* and *The Age of Empire*). On the other hand, there is the kind of micro-analysis which Edward Thompson conducts in *Whigs and Hunters*, and Charles Van Onselen in *The Seed Is Mine* (a book to which I shall return), where a specific episode, or even an individual life, is examined.

Marxism's ability to switch from widescreen epic to narrow focus close-up reflects its nature as a theory of history. Historical materialism identifies two main mechanisms of social transformation: first, the tendency for the forces and relations of production to come into conflict with one another, causing the entire social system to go into crisis; secondly, the class struggle between exploiters and exploited—'the now hidden, now open' fight which Marx calls 'the immediate motive force of history' and which develops on the basis of the structural contradictions within the mode of production. This theoretical framework allows Marxist historians to deal in entire historical epochs; it also permits them to home in on the ways in which resistance to exploitation is present in the very grain of social life.

It is because it can operate at both macro- and micro-levels 31 that Marxism is superior to the kind of structuralist history pursued by the *Annales* school. Braudel famously dismissed events as 'surface disturbances, crests of foam that the tides of history carry on their strong backs'.[20] Historical change thus takes the form of gradual, imperceptible transformations of the underlying structures. This objectivist stance sometimes encourages scholars influenced by Braudel to see history as following an essentially cyclical course. Thus Giovanni Arrighi denies that the history of capitalism is a process of development: rather, the past 700 years have seen the repetition four times over of a 'systemic cycle of accumulation', in which are to be found 'patterns of recurrence and evolution'—for example, each cycle culminates in a phase of financial expansion.[21] Because Marxist historians understand that some events—namely, revolutions—can affect structures, initiating qualitative social transformations, they are able to reinstate agency, giving it sometimes a decisive role in the historical process.

Currently, however, Marxism is under attack in both registers. At the macro-level, Weberian sociologists such as Michael Mann and W G Runciman have constructed alternative theories of history which seek to cover the whole of the human past: the first volume of Mann's *The Sources of Social Power* is subtitled *A History of Power From the Beginning to 1760*. Meanwhile, postmodernists in effect counterpose Marxism and micro-history. Jean-François Lyotard claims that the postmodern condition arises from the collapse of the 'grand narratives', of the attempts by the Enlightenment, Hegel, and Marx to offer comprehensive interpretations of the whole of human history. The fall of the grand narratives creates the space in which what Lyotard calls 'the little narrative' [petit récit], 'the quintessential form of imaginative invention', can flourish.[22]

Postmodernism indeed has developed a positive cult of the fragmentary. 'Let us make war on totality,' says Lyotard.[23] Gyanendra Pandey, a leading member of the *Subaltern Studies* group of historians, who have evolved astonishingly quickly from Marxism to postmodernism, writes:

> What the historians call a 'fragment'—a weaver's diary, a collection of poems by an unknown poet (and to those we might add all those literatures of India that Macaulay condemned, creation myths and women's songs, family genealogies and local traditions)—is of central importance in challenging the state's construction of history, in

thinking other histories and marking those contested spaces through which particular unities are sought to be constituted and others broken up.[24]

These two kinds of attack on Marxism have more in common than might appear at first glance. For both share certain theoretical assumptions that can be traced back ultimately to the thought of Friedrich Nietzsche. Nietzsche saw reality as a plurality of rival power-centres struggling for domination over one another. Following him Michel Foucault, a key influence on postmodernist historians, formulated the idea that every society is constituted by an 'apparatus' of 'power-knowledge': resistance must remain fragmented in order to avoid incorporation into this apparatus. Max Weber was also deeply influenced by Nietzsche. His contemporary followers such as Mann and Runciman argue that the 'sources' or 'modes of distribution' of power are inherently plural and autonomous of one another: the economy, therefore, cannot have 'ultimate primacy' over the others.

The uses of micro-history

Marxism can, as it happens, deal with both of these challenges. As far as the macro-level is concerned, I have tried to show elsewhere that Mann's attempts to demonstrate that military and ideological power are autonomous of the forces and relations of production are unsuccessful.[25] As for postmodernism, its claim essentially to appropriate microhistory for itself is really the most astonishing piece of effrontery given the existence of books like *Whigs and Hunters*.

Carlo Ginzburg is one of the most outstanding contemporary micro-historians. His best known work, *The Cheese and The Worms*, is a wonderful attempt at recovering popular beliefs in early modern Europe, based on the records of the Inquisition's interrogations of Menocchio, a Friulian miller, at the end of the 16th century. Ginzburg is no Marxist, but rather an eccentric sort of structuralist. Yet he has expressed his fury at postmodernist attempts to claim micro-history as its own. Work such as his, Ginzburg says, involved 'an explicit rejection of the sceptical implications (postmodernist if you will) so largely present in European and American historiography of the 1980s and early 1990s'. Micro-history involves 'the insistence on context, exactly

33

the opposite of the isolated contemplation of the fragmentary' recommended by postmodernists.[26]

The stress Ginzburg lays here on the importance of context is crucial. The minute description of detail for its own sake is meaningless. The postmodernist cult of the fragment bears a suspicious resemblance to the traditional empiricist hostility to historical theory. Both Cold War liberals like Karl Popper and G R Elton and contemporary postmodernists like Lyotard and Pandey seek to ban an attempt to understand societies as developing totalities because they believe that such large-scale theorising leads inevitably to totalitarian dictatorship: the main difference is that Popper at least offered bad arguments in support of this claim whereas postmodernists simply assert it dogmatically.

Yet what the best kind of micro-history does is, through the close study of the particular, to reveal something of the nature of the larger whole. Charles Van Onselen's book *The Seed is Mine* is a good example of how this can be done. Van Onselen was a leading figure in the brilliant generation of Marxist historians who transformed our understanding of modern South Africa in the 1970s. It is an example of the larger tragedy of the South African left that in recent years Van Onselen has been one of a group of senior white academics at Wits University in Johannesburg who have resisted the demands for reform from black students and staff. But, however repugnant the political stands he has taken at Wits, the fact remains that Van Onselen has written a remarkable historical work.

The Seed is Mine is about Kas Maine, an African sharecropper in the south western Transvaal. Born in 1894, Maine struggled throughout much of the 20th century to find land on which he could grow crops like maize and sorghum. Given that most of the land was own by whites, this inevitably meant making sharecropping agreements with white farmers. The space within which someone like Maine—an efficient black producer, indeed a would-be capitalist entrepreneur—could exist became ever narrower. The increasingly capitalist nature of South African agriculture conspired with the segregationist policies of the state, beginning with the Native Lands Act 1913 and culminating in the forced removals pursued by the National Party regime after 1948, to squeeze him out. By the time he died in 1985, Maine had been driven onto one of the rural dumping grounds in the Bophuthatswana 'homeland' which the apartheid state has set aside for 'surplus' Africans.

But Van Onselen's book, based on extensive interviews, does more than reconstruct the life of an indomitable survivor, a character who could have stepped out of one of Brecht's plays, refusing, even in the face of old age and the disintegration of his family caused by the pressures of apartheid and capitalism, to give up. Through telling Maine's story, Van Onselen reveals larger patterns. One of the most striking is the relation of interdependence that, contrary to racial ideology, sharecropping developed between white and black on the *platteland* fabled as a stronghold of Afrikaner nationalism:

> Farming-on-the-halves facilitated inter-racial social practices that transcended the clauses of the economic contract binding the parties together. With no great economic distance separating them, and with both parties far from their more densely populated cultural hinterlands, white landlords and black sharecroppers developed a modus vivendi embracing shared ideas about dress, health, justice, language, production, recreation and religious life. Poor Afrikaners emerged from the comparative seclusion of this shared experience far more 'Africanised' than their protestations would lead one to believe, while better off Africans were far more 'Afrikanerised' than cultural purists are willing to concede. Class stroked away at the fibres of the emerging culture until it, like the fur on the cat, was best reconciled with the underlying shape.[27]

Tracing an individual life thus allows Van Onselen to uncover larger truths about the interrelations of race and class in apartheid South Africa. In this respect, his book is exemplary. Micro-history at its best does not celebrate the fragment for its own sake, but rather examines details as a way of gaining insight into the whole. Exploring the particular leads here towards, not away from, the totality.

The need for total history

Contemporary intellectual fashion is very hostile to totalisation— towards trying to set particular phenomena in the larger context of a social whole. Thus Edward Said, whose book *Orientalism* helped to inspire the version of postmodernism known as postcolonial theory, writes, 'I am temperamentally and philosophically opposed to vast system building or totalistic theories of human history.' He goes on, however, immediately to add, 'But I must

35

say that having studied and indeed lived within the modern empires, I am struck by how constantly expanding, how inexorably integrative they were'.[28] Why the past tense? Think of the successive crises in the Gulf, or the current race, involving virtually every major capitalist power, for the oil of the Caspian Sea.

And that is precisely the point. The necessity of totalisation arises, not, as postmodernists would argue, from some totalitarian urge to dominate and control, but from the fact that, as it happens, the capitalist mode of production, under which we all live, operates according to a logic that is in the most literal sense global, incorporating and subordinating every aspect of social life everywhere to the drive to accumulate. We may not like the fact that capitalism is a totality, but the truth is that it is, and if we want to achieve a world is that freer, more open and plural, we had better start to understand it as such.

'Always historicise!' the Marxist critic Fredric Jameson once wrote.[29] And that is right: understanding things involves setting them in their historical context. But one should add, 'Always totalise!' Reconstructing the historical context requires understanding it as a network of social relations which constitute a contradictory whole operating according to a distinctive logic of crisis, struggle, and transformation.[30]

To put it more concretely, it seems to me that Marxist history has at least to aspire to be total history in three ways. First of all, it should seek to combine history from above with history from below, to study the organisation and strategies of the dominant class as well as the life and struggles of the oppressed and exploited. John Saville's study in his book *1848* of the British state's response to Chartism during the revolutionary year of 1848 is a relatively rare example of this. Secondly, Marxist history should strive to integrate the objective context—the structural tendencies of the mode of production—with the subjective experience of those on whose labour everything depends. Ste Croix's *The Class Struggle in the Ancient Greek World* is a particularly remarkable attempt to bring together structure and subjectivity. Thirdly, in exploring the modern world, Marxist history has to locate the national within the international: as Sam Ashman shows elsewhere in this volume, one of the great weaknesses of the historians who emerged from the Communist Party was their tendency to approach history in largely English, national terms.

These prescriptions may seem like an impossibly tall order.

But there are works which achieve this—above all Trotsky's great *History of the Russian Revolution*. Not everyone can be Trotsky, but, as I have suggested, even work whose focus is very specific and localised can still have an *orientation* towards total history as defined above. This is true, albeit in a rather eccentric way, of Peter Linebaugh's *The London Hanged*, which integrates the 'thanatocracy' of the 18th century English state—its reliance on the systematic use of public execution as a form of social power—with both the developing patterns of capital accumulation in the Atlantic economy and different forms of class organisation and resistance.

Beyond history from below

Marxism constitutes, in my view, the best approach to the understanding of history, in part because of its ability to operate at both the macro- and the micro-level, to explore long term tendencies and to uncover resistance on the small scale. Yet affirming the superiority of historical materialism should not be confused with a simple defence of the 'history from below' tradition in general and Edward Thompson's work in particular. Such, however, has been the response of many Marxist historians in the face of the postmodernist onslaught.

Of course, there is much to value, to defend, and indeed to celebrate in the 'history from below' tradition. But there is nevertheless, particularly in the context of the kind of issues raised by the 'linguistic turn', one crucial weakness in Thompson's version of Marxism. This is his tendency, at least in his theoretical pronouncements, to equate class with experience. Thus he calls class 'a self defining historical formation, which men and women make out of their own experience of struggle'.[31] This way of thinking about class is an understandable reaction to crude Stalinist treatments according to which, as Thompson puts it, 'the working class was the more or less spontaneous generation of new productive forces and relations'.[32] But his privileging the *experience* of historical processes confronts Thompson with profound difficulties.[33] The trouble with experience is that it is, by definition, subjective. To describe how someone experienced an event is to describe that event from that person's point of view. In principle, therefore, everyone's experience is as valid as everyone else's.

But if all experiences are equally valid, how should one respond

37

to a book like Linda Colley's *Britons*? Colley takes the period which Thompson made his own —the 18th and early 19th centuries— but offers a very different picture. This was, she claims, a period, not of riot and rebellion, but of the construction of modern British national identity on the basis of mass patriotism forged during the British state's century of war with France. The artisans and labourers who rallied to the Volunteers to defend Britain against French invasion in the 1790s and 1800s were, Colley suggests, more representative than Thompson's pro-Jacobin radicals in the Corresponding Societies. Indeed, she claims, 'In Great Britain, as in other major European powers, it was training in arms under the auspices of the state that was the most common collective working class experience in the late 18th and early 19th centuries, not labour in a factory, or membership of a radical political organisation or an illegal trade union'.[34]

Thompson responded in one of his last published pieces by fairly robustly reaffirming his view of English society at the turn of the 19th century, but he clearly had difficulty in showing why his account of the period was more accurate than Colley's. The question is one that cannot be resolved simply by comparing different experiences. Yet Thompson compounds the problem by declaring, ' "Class" was perhaps overworked in the 1960s and 1970s and it has become merely boring. It is a concept long past its sell-by date'.[35]

Thompson's followers have been less willing to sell the pass in this way, but by hanging onto his subjective definition of class they are unable to come up with an effective response to post-modernism. Thus the Canadian Trotskyist historian Bryan Palmer argues that 'class relations are, in origin, economic relations rooted in the capitalist process of accumulation, whereby one social stratum expropriates surplus from another.' Consequently, 'class takes on its most clear-cut objective presence in the epoch of classical industrial capitalism, stretching from the triumph of the Industrial Revolution in the mid-19th century to the high-water mark of monopoly capitalism just prior to World War Two.' As a result of the subsequent 'decay of industrial capitalism', 'the place of class is obscured' in contemporary capitalism. As for 'precapitalist epochs...class is less of a presence, socially and economically, and more of a metaphor encompassing a range of tensions, antagonisms, and conflicts'.[36]

38   The history of hitherto existing society turns out not to be the

history of class struggle after all. Palmer's talk of class as a 'presence' makes clear that he thinks of it primarily as a visible way of organising society. Class analysis extends only so far as class is visible, that is, as people explicitly think and act in terms of class. It is Joyce who brings out how the logic of this kind of equation of class with class consciousness leads to it vanishing altogether:

> As Thompson argues, classes do not have pre-given identities, a 'true' consciousness. This is so. They acquire consciousness of class identity in historical eventuation, very often in struggle. But the problem is to know what class identity looks like, and where it starts and stops. One cannot simply ascribe a class consciousness to the social struggles of subordinate groups because they are in struggle.[37]

Historical materialism is sustainable only if a sharp distinction is drawn between class consciousness and class itself, understood as an objective relationship arising from the relations of production themselves. Ste Croix provides the best single discussion of this point. Calling class 'the collective social expression of the fact that exploitation is embodied in a social structure', he defines a class as 'a group of persons in a community identified by their position in the whole system of social production, defined above all according to the relationship (primarily in terms of ownership or control) to the conditions of production (that is to say, the means of labour of production) and to other classes.' Class thus understood is different from class consciousness or overt conflict. Indeed, Ste Croix argues, 'To adopt the very common conception of class struggle which refuses to regard it as such unless it includes *class consciousness* and *active political conflict* (as some Marxists do) is to water it down to the point where it virtually disappears in many situations'.[38]

Conceiving class in this way as an objective relationship rooted in the process of exploitation does not require that we ignore all the aspects of human existence highlighted by the 'linguistic turn'—discourse, subjectivity, culture, and so on. On the contrary, Marxist class theory provides a framework within which all this can be understood, not as a free-floating process, but as the ways in which human beings located in contradictory relations of production seek to make sense of the world, and develop strategies for coping with, and sometimes for changing it.[39]

39

Conclusion

Historians from a Marxist background are sometimes tempted to find some common ground with postmodernism. For example, Geoff Eley and Keith Neild offer a rebuttal of Joyce's wilder claims from what they describe as 'a perspective sympathetic to the discourse of post-structuralism and postmodernism'.[40] This search for compromise seems to me mistaken. Even when dissociated from textual idealism, postmodernism is based on a set of assumptions (deriving ultimately from Nietzsche) which treat social domination as a permanent and ineradicable feature of human existence. Marxism, by contrast, looks toward a society where exploitation and oppression have been abolished.

Ultimately, then, like the controversies over the French and Russian revolutions, the debate about postmodernism in history is not about the past, but about the future. What is at issue is whether or not social revolution—socialist revolution—is both feasible and desirable. Classical Marxism answers this question strongly in the affirmative. There is a close connection here between political objective and scientific method. Marxism seeks to understand capitalism as a totality the better to concentrate the forces of revolt against it.

CHAPTER 3

Women's history

Lindsey German

Until relatively recently the study of women's history was largely unknown. That has changed in the last two decades and it is now taught on specific courses in colleges and is the subject of large numbers of studies. To some right wingers, this is simply the result of political correctness in the colleges. But rather we should see this development as part of a particular set of historical circumstances which have allowed women to act more freely than in any previous generation. This includes large numbers of women gaining access to higher education and at least some of them developing an interest in what role women have played in history.

We should not be surprised by this. The rise of specific interest in women's history has coincided with dramatic social changes in women's lives. This has been true particularly in two periods in the 20th century when there was very swift and dramatic change in how women worked, lived and perceived themselves. The first period was around the First World War when the blossoming of women's history was quite dramatic. The suffragette movement which erupted before the war had a big impact on a layer of educated and middle class women, who became radicalised around a range of issues. The position of these women had changed considerably within the space of one or two generations. Whereas for much of the 19th century women from such class backgrounds were not expected to work, or to engage in any serious education, by the 1880s and 1890s this was beginning to change. New girls' schools teaching serious subjects were being established, women were being allowed—in a very limited way—into higher education, and for the first time a small number were

41

being treated as individuals with a role outside the home. The rise of what was called the new woman—independent, radical and sexually liberated—coincided with this development. In addition, middle class women began to engage in paid work, for example, as typewriters—what today we would call secretaries or typists.

Women began looking at issues from new vantage points, especially that tiny minority which had access to universities or to some sort of research. It was in this context that a layer of new women historians developed, many associated with the gradualist socialist intellectual group, the Fabian Society. These women tended to write social history, concentrating on the history of women in and around work, or on more sociological studies about the conditions under which working women lived in contemporary Britain. So Clementina Black wrote *Married Women Working* and Maud Pember Reeves' *Round about a Pound a Week* which described contemporary working class life, although we would now view them obviously as historical documents. After the First World War there were a number of historical studies: Barbara Drake's pathbreaking book in 1920 on women in the trade unions; Alice Clarke on women in the 17th century (1919); and in 1930 Ivy Pinchbeck's *Women Workers and the Industrial Revolution*, which is still one of the best books on the history of women workers and which helps develop an understanding of what happened to women in the crucial 100 years from 1750 to 1850 with the Industrial Revolution and the development of modern capitalism.

These books were, however, largely unknown to or ignored by later generations; access to them was confined to a tiny number of people. Indeed, when the historian Keith Thomas, teaching at Oxford in the 1950s, tried to organise a series of lectures on women in the 17th century 'his colleagues found the subject bizarre and the students simply did not turn up to listen'.[1] There were books written on a number of subjects relating to women in those years but the marginalisation of women's history only changed significantly with the emergence of the modern women's movement in the 1960s, following the second great period of change in women's lives, that period of the post-war boom from the 1940s to the 1960s when women found access to jobs, education and greater individual freedom on a scale previously regarded as utopian. The existence of a social movement around women especially in the US but also in Britain gave added impetus to the study of history, so by the early 1970s a new generation of women writers was coming to the fore.

The title of one of the most popular books of the period, *Hidden from History* by Sheila Rowbotham, which detailed an overview of women's role in history, seemed to encapsulate the feeling of many: that we were now viewing for the first time the role of women as active participants in history.[2] The nature of the subject matter and the period and social background from which these writers sprang meant that many were influenced by the left, and were in turn attracted to the ideas summarised by the development of history from below and of labour history. This was history from the point of view of the hitherto largely unknown and usually underprivileged—and this sort of history also began to redress the balance of historical study in favour of women.

All the faults of bourgeois history which dominated teaching in schools and universities prior to the 1960s—history from the top down, the history of a few famous people—were highlighted in relation to women's history. I left school in 1969 and my view was that there were three categories of women in history: there were queens, there was the braying mob—women involved in bread riots or knitting at the guillotine during the French Revolution—and there were the suffragettes. These different elements were supposed to represent the sum of women's historical experience.

With the development of new ways of looking at history from the point of view of the participants a new and hitherto virtually unknown dimension of women's role opened up. We began to learn that the match girls' strike of 1888, which was almost exclusively composed of women, marked the beginning of the struggle for the New Unionism among the unskilled and previously unorganised. The period of mass strikes known as the Great Unrest in the years before the First World War also saw the mass involvement of women workers. In the summer of 1911 there was an explosion of women's strikes in south and east London especially in industries connected with food processing. The real story of the fight for the suffrage was also much more interesting and complicated than had been hitherto taught in schools, as the new histories on, for example, the northern working class suffragists showed. The suffragists were more constitutional in their aims than the suffragettes and saw their role as campaigning for

43

change within and around the emerging Labour Party and within the unions, especially the female dominated textile unions.[3]

Writing history about women, especially from a feminist point of view, was relatively straightforward while it remained at the level of description. Once it moved beyond that it very rapidly brought the authors up against a theoretical problem. Change in women's lives and change in broader society had to be explained with reference to wider forces, but many feminists rejected a view of history which saw changes in women's lives coming from the same forces as those things which changed men's lives. Instead they looked to patriarchy theory to underpin their analysis of women's oppression. In this context, 19th century working class women's history became a battlefield where various writers fought to try to establish what the roots of women's oppression really were. In particular, a debate opened up about whether it was in the interests of male workers to maintain women's oppression and if therefore the fight for liberation was not simply against capital but against men as well.

There were those who claimed that patriarchy was just an ideological phenomenon, that there were two separate spheres, 'the economic mode of capitalism and the ideological mode of patriarchy'[4] which were completely autonomous and which needed separate strategies in order to confront them. This argument was essentially that, regardless of what material changes happened in the lives of working men and women, the ideas of women's oppression endured in the form of patriarchy, which coexisted alongside capitalism. The political conclusion which followed from this analysis was the need for totally separate struggles against capitalism on the one hand and against patriarchy on the other—hence the need for a separate women's movement to organise against patriarchy.

There was, however, a fundamental weakness with this theory: women's lives had changed beyond all recognition under capitalism and were still changing. How could such material changes take place and this not affect the ideas which people had in their heads? The theory seemed to accept that there could be a complete transformation in the family, in the sort of work people did, in the way that they lived, without this in any way affecting ideas of male domination or women's subordination. The theory was only sustainable if the development of ideas was regarded as completely separate from the development of society, and many

44

people could spot the weakness with this argument. It was relatively easy for Marxists to argue that such a theory was idealist, starting from the ideas in people's heads, rather than the circumstances which created them.

Much harder to deal with, however, was an argument put forward by the US feminist Heidi Hartmann, who wrote an influential article which later became part of a collection of essays called *The Unhappy Marriage of Marxism and Feminism*.[5] The theme of the essay was to provide a material explanation of patriarchy. Hartmann understood that it was not adequate to explain patriarchy simply by the backward ideas in men's heads. Instead she argued that the material reason for its continued existence, despite the many changes which capitalism had wrought in the lives of women, lay in an alliance between (male) labour and capital to ensure that the family was strengthened, that women were kept out of better paid and often the only available work, and that the family wage led to a family structure with a male breadwinner on whom the woman and children were totally dependent.

Hartmann argued that the material basis for patriarchy was 'men's control over women's labour power'.[6] During the 19th century a Faustian bargain was struck between male labour and capital. In return for protective legislation, which excluded women and children from certain sorts of work, most notably coal mining, and a family wage paid to the male—in other words a wage sufficient to keep not only the worker but also his family without any other members of the family having to go out to work—male workers agreed to women being pushed out of work. This gave them a privileged position in the workplace, where the monopoly of skilled and better paid jobs stayed with men, and a privileged position in the home as the pivot of the male breadwinner family. The capitalists in return developed an increasingly skilled workforce, and had to lay out relatively little in costs of reproduction for the existing and future generations of workers, since their welfare and upbringing were carried by the family itself. This was to the detriment of the women in particular, who lost the ability to become independent wage earners especially after marriage, and who had their oppression reinforced by their dependence on the man in the home.

This argument can be shown to be false in many respects as I will try to demonstrate below. However, it contained one important grain of truth. It attempted a plausible explanation of the

45

continued existence of the working class family in circumstances where its very future had seemed under threat and therefore seemed to challenge other explanations, especially that put forward by Karl Marx and Frederick Engels in the 1840s, who argued that the oppression of women was bound up with the development of class society, and with it the institution of the family.

Marx and Engels argued that the needs of any particular class society led to the development of a particular form of family, which changed as the mode of production itself changed. Capitalist society, divided as it was into two major classes, created two quite different sorts of family. The family of the bourgeoisie was based on private property. The experience of working class life was very different. The proletariat possessed no property. In addition, every member of the family was pulled into the labour market in the early years of capitalism, especially in the textile industry. This had the effect of destroying the old patriarchal family which had existed before the factory system. Marx and Engels therefore believed that the tendency of the working class family under capitalism was to disappear.

The fact is, however, that this did not happen. The tendency which appeared so strong to Engels when he wrote about the breakdown of family life in *The Condition of the Working Class in England* did not continue. Certainly in the second half of the 19th century the working class family as an institution was strengthened, and with it came a whole series of attitudes which tended to reinforce women's subordinate role. It is this phenomenon for which Hartmann's analysis attempts to provide an explanation. Unfortunately, the historical record tends to show that as a matter of fact she was wrong on all the major counts.

Protective legislation

In the first half of the 19th century protective legislation was concetrated on two aspects of work: the reduction of hours for certain classes of workers, most notably children, and the exclusion of women and children from certain jobs. Hartmann argued that protective legislation was fought for by men inside the working class, alongside sections of the capitalist class, in order to exclude cheap female or child competition and that this gave to men inside the working class the monopoly of the good jobs. She also claimed it reinforced a sexual division of labour which discriminated against women. In fact, the purpose of the protective legislation from the point of view of workers was generally to improve the conditions of working class life. The Factory Act of 1833 which restricted hours and night work applied only to children; it was only in 1844 that subsequent legislation included women, who were prevented from working more than 12 hours or from working nights.

The major opposition to restricting hours came from the employers, although increasingly sections of the bourgeoisie came to see some value in restricting hours if in exchange it was able to employ a more skilled and healthy—and therefore more productive—workforce. The restriction of women working in coal mines was only introduced just before the introduction of the 1842 legislation which had developed from an inquiry into child labour in the mines, mainly as a result, it seems, of 'numerous petitions on the subject which were addressed to parliament from Lancashire and Yorkshire towns'.[7]

It is also wrong to see the legislation as having a major effect on women's work nationally. Even before the legislation women only worked in certain sorts of mining and therefore only in certain areas: the West Riding of Yorkshire, Lancashire and Cheshire, the east of Scotland and South Wales.[8] Even within these areas the number of women employed was often relatively small—for example, in Yorkshire only 22 women per 1,000 men worked in the mines.[9] In most areas men and women were simply not in direct competition with each other for jobs. While the exclusion of women from work obviously had a major impact in areas where there was such competition, it cannot explain why the whole of the working class developed a division of labour which discriminated against women.

The unions

A similar point can be made regarding the unions. The vast majority of workers in Britain, both men and women, were not in trade unions throughout most of the 19th century. Indeed, the unions were phenomenally weak in most areas of work. As late as 1870 only 400,000 workers out of 11 million in the workforce belonged to unions—a much smaller proportion than today when between a quarter and a third of workers are in unions. The two major areas of women's employment were in domestic service—where there were

47

no unions—and textiles, which was highly unionised and where women played a full role. Many of the other areas of unionisation traditionally employed either very few or no women at all, since the early unions, where they existed, were nearly always based on craft skills. It should be stressed that these trades tended to be highly exclusive, but they were exclusive of the majority of men as well as of women. The idea that these bodies could be responsible for the shaping of women's employment attributes to them an influence and power which they simply did not have.

The family wage

If Hartmann's argument that male workers received a family wage in return for pushing women back into the home is true, then working class men would have gained some sort of material benefit from women's oppression. Yet it is hard to sustain the argument that most men did receive a family wage. Many studies of working class income in the second half of the 19th century show that the male earnings alone were simply not sufficient to cover the costs of reproduction (food, clothing, housing etc) in most working class families. In addition to this, substantial numbers of married women continued to work outside the home throughout the 19th century (as well as the large numbers who supplemented family income by taking in boarders, washing or other sorts of service work). So Clementina Black points to a number of industries where married women's work was central; and in textiles a third of the women workers in the 1860s were married.[10]

Perhaps most devastating of all to Hartmann's thesis is the evidence put forward by Jane Humphries about women's role in the workforce. Humphries shows that in the years immediately following the introduction of protective legislation women's workforce participation rose. It remained high in the 1860s and 1870s. It was only very late in the 19th century that women's workforce participation appeared to decline—and this was a trend which continued into the first two or three decades of the 20th century. Part of the problem with discussing these questions lies in the inaccuracy or non-comparability of some of the figures, including some of the census returns, which seem to have underestimated the number of women working at certain times. By making certain allowances and adjustments, however, the figures used by Humphries (from a study by Higgs) show that 'female activity rates in 1851-71 were almost certainly higher than any that were recorded again until after the Second World War, and perhaps even until the 1960s'.[11]

This shows that, whatever the truth about the removal of women from work, it did not coincide with industrialisation or with the capitalist development of the early and mid-19th century. This alone knocks a hole in the Hartmann thesis, which equates women's subordination with the advent of industrial capitalism and the male working class. Evidence even for the later period is very mixed, with some writers believing that women's work, and part time work in particular, has been underestimated by historians, thus systematically down-playing married women's work.[12]

More importantly, however, even if we accept Jane Humphries' analysis that around the end of the 19th and the beginning of the 20th centuries women's work outside the home did decline compared with previous decades, there is no need to accept patriarchy theory's capitalist-male worker conspiracy in order to explain it. Humphries herself puts forward a number of reasons why women did not enter certain jobs: geographical mobility was much harder for both married and single women; there was also a question of physical strength in certain industries.[13] She argues that, if questions of the family wage and union strength had any influence on women's work, they did not do so until much later than the period usually designated by feminist historians. Other factors, such as the marriage bar in certain industries (where married women had to give up work they had previously done while single), were also instrumental in preventing women from working in larger numbers until the 1930s.[14]

The questions of when, how and why women went out to work at various periods and in particular geographical areas is complicated and controversial. However, the starting point for anyone trying to understand the development of part of the working class has to be the rejection of any conspiracy theory in favour of understanding the way in which the labour market works. This is really impossible to do without some theory of class. The accumulation of capital is the motor of capitalism and with it goes the exploitation of the working class. The drive to accumulation means that capital tends use differences of gender, race or nationality to create further divisions—but the key question for capital is which group of workers can be exploited most efficiently. The particular work patterns of women have to be seen in this context. Historically women have often played the role of a reserve army of labour. This was most obviously the case during the two world wars, when women were drawn into the workforce to replace men who had been conscripted to fight. But it can also be argued that women have played the role of a reserve army in the post-war years, not by being a *disposable* army—they are now clearly a permanent and increasing part of the workforce—but by their employment lowering the level of wages overall. In this sense the capitalist class today often seems to prefer to employ women workers, seeing them as more flexible and willing to accept lower pay.

We also have to look at the 19th century in a political context, because the shape which the British working class took was determined by political as well as economic considerations. The defeat of Chartism by the middle of the century and the rapid growth of British capitalism and empire in the decades which immediately followed meant that the working class movement developed along narrow lines and accepted much of bourgeois ideology. In the view of Dorothy Thompson something happened to the movement in those years which led to ideological retreat and the development of reactionary ideas around, for example, the family, and that this was coupled with the withdrawal of women from public life and protest.[15] Frederick Engels described how the workers had no political independence from the bourgeoisie:

> You ask me what the English workers think about colonial policy.
> Well, exactly the same as they think about politics in general: the
> same as the bourgeoisie think.[16]

The defeat of Chartism, a movement of the working class based essentially on universalist and inclusivist ideas, had a huge impact. This defeat alongside the growing wealth of British capitalism and its pre-eminence among its rivals allowed the British capitalist class to ride any protests or discontent over the ensuing decades. The depression of the 1870s and 1880s changed this, and led to the development first of organised socialist ideas and then of the first mass unions of the unskilled; nonetheless, the development of the working class had already been marked by its narrow and sectional outlook, and even the big general struggles were distorted by this. This affected the working class family. It was in theory possible for working class men and women to fight for equal access to work for men and women, and for an equal division of labour within the home. In practice the division of labour at work acted to the advantage of men. There is little question that where women had a choice, once they had children, of whether to work or not, many of them saw staying at home as preferable.

This was hardly surprising. Conditions in Britain were appalling for working class families in the years after the Industrial Revolution. Child labour led to terrible levels of infant mortality and injury. Even after its abolition the conditions in which their mothers (and fathers) had to live still produced terrible suffering. Long hours of work and high levels of poverty led to neglect, poor diet, malnutrition of babies and so on. Parents who worked long hours found that they could not care for their children properly. Increasingly working class families began to connect improvements in their living standards with the withdrawal of children and increasingly women from the labour market. This was not of course the only way of improving the health and living standards of working class families, but it was clearly the option which appeared most realistic. The limited aspirations and narrow horizons of many in the working class at that time did not lead towards collective solutions such as publicly provided childcare—and this was certainly not advocated by the ruling class. Therefore the preferred option became the withdrawal of women from paid work and the demand for a family wage to provide for all members of the family. However much this remained far from reality for most workers, and however much the aspiration was shared by both men and women in the working class, the fact that it was women who were expected to withdraw from work was clearly a defeat for women inside the working class and a setback in terms of ideas for the working class as a whole.

The collective and the individual

The relationship between collective exploitation and individual oppression is mediated by the family which is itself a product of class society. It is here that we have to start when analysing why women remain oppressed. Some earlier feminist historians were also socialists and so accepted some of this analysis. In *Woman's Consciousness, Man's World*, Sheila Rowbotham wrote:

I consider the solution to exploitation and oppression to be communism, despite the hollow resonance the word has acquired. It seems to me that the cultural and economic liberation of women is inseparable from the creation of a society in which all people no longer have their lives stolen from them, and in which the conditions of their production and reproduction will no longer be distorted and held back by the subordination of sex, race and class.[17]

However this was not the analysis taken up by most involved in feminist history. Indeed, even socialist feminists began to retreat from these ideas. The Communist Party women historians in particular were faced with a contradiction: they were trying to build a women's movement based on all women having something in common while at the same time being part of an organisation which based its analysis at least partly on class. They also had to explain why in the so called socialist countries women were as oppressed as anywhere else. The theory of patriarchy appeared to overcome these contradictions by assuming that the fight against oppression was quite separate from that against exploitation and so two separate revolutions were needed. By the late 1970s this theory was dominant inside the women's movement.

The ideas of feminism led many socialists towards patriarchy theory. Even Sheila Rowbotham, who does not accept the theory of patriarchy, theorised women in the household as operating a mode within a mode of production. 'In the relation between husband and wife there is an exchange of services which resembled the bond between man and man in feudalism. The woman essentially serves the man in exchange for care and protection'.[18] Even by the early 1970s this was not a particularly accurate view of how most people lived, but nonetheless this was an attempt to apply a Marxist analysis to justify the idea that there had to be separate revolutions. It is a short step from here to accepting the whole theory of patriarchy.

Patriarchy theory also led in an apolitical direction which said that women's history should be looked at from the point of view of women who live in all classes. The radical feminists, who became much more dominant in the late 1970s and early 1980s, moved away from any idea of social history to history about any women who were strong, interesting or famous, and these women tended not to be the workers, poor peasants or people who suffered most in society, but the people who had access to education or to wealth.

This led to quite reactionary women's history, for example, praising the various attempts by some women to secure the prohibition of alcohol and the prohibition of prostitution because of sexual diseases. Some of the campaigners in these areas were complete reactionaries, the 19th century equivalent of the moral right in the US today. Yet they were now regarded as somehow fighting against women's oppression.[19]

Even among socialist feminists who stayed on the left, history tended to avoid the decisive turning points in the class struggle and class polarisation such as the English Revolution, the French Revolution, the Paris Commune and the Great Unrest—periods when people did not just act as they had done for generations, but started to act in a very different way. There is a different analysis of why they acted and different interpretations of what they did, but nonetheless any attempt to move towards simply looking at everyday life where nothing much changes is a retreat from trying to understand women's history.

There are many good studies which examine housework, marriage and other 'family' centred issues. For example, a very good book by Diana Gittins talks about fertility in different sorts of working class communities. She shows how textile workers had very low rates of fertility for working class women because they had a much greater chance of a job and were much more likely to be employed. The women who did not have much prospect of work, for example in the coal mining areas such as South Wales, tended to be the ones who stayed at home and had large families.[20] However, studies about why people had certain sorts of family, or why they wore particular clothes or cooked particular food, have to be put in a specific context. Beneath any of these supposedly everyday questions lie material changes in society and in economics. For example, women dressed and acted in quite specific and often quite new ways during the Second World War in Britain. But their tastes in music and fashion can only be understood in the context of very new freedoms especially for young women, such as working in 'male' jobs, earning their own income and living away from home before marriage.

Whereas when the 1960s wave of feminist history began there was a strong Marxist and materialist flavour to it, today that is

53

not the case. Postmodernist theory means that we are told there is no hierarchy of discourse, nothing can be more important than anything else, and there is certainly no real attempt to come to terms with change for women. The influence of postmodernism is most obvious in the rewriting of the history of the women's movement itself. There is supposedly a younger generation who are claiming that feminism was all about not wearing lipstick or dressing unfashionably. This was never true—it was never about whether people wore makeup or not. It was about people refusing to be restricted by these kinds of images. Anyone who knows anything about the history of the women's movement will know that the whole question of sexuality was an absolutely central component to it—whether you are talking about the right to choose over abortion, or protests over women's and men's college accommodation being segregated, or the writing on the myth of the vaginal orgasm. The consequence of removing class from history in women's politics has been instrumental in stressing this individualistic view of women's liberation. Once you start saying that it does not matter, that class is not a component, or all women have something in common, then you develop ideas which lead to a retreat from the idea of complete liberation. In countries such as Britain or the US where there are a minority of women, about 15 percent, who do have a lot of individual freedom financially, socially and so on, then the argument goes that if this could be raised to 30 percent then everything would be all right. It is only a short step from this to arguing that the other 70 percent have only themselves to blame if they cannot achieve such heights, that it is the fault of the women at the bottom—the single parents or the unemployed—that they find themselves in this position.

All of this misses the most important point to understand about women today: that we have undergone in a lifetime a complete revolution in the way that women live and work. Some statistics from the US tell us a great deal: one is the changing composition of US households between 1960 and 1995. In 1960 there were 85.7 percent family households—today there are 70 percent. Married couples made up 74.8 percent in 1960—today it is 54.4 percent; married couples with children 47.5 percent—today it is 25.5 percent. Births per 100 women in 1960 (by the end of child bearing age) were 345—today the figure is 205; women aged 25 to 34 currently not married were only 11.5 percent in 1960—today it is 41 percent. Out of wedlock births were 5.3 percent in 1960—

today they are 31 percent; and families headed by single mothers were 9.9 percent—now the figure is 23.6 percent.[21]

This is not just a small social shift, this is a fundamental change in women's lives, how they live, work and their attitudes, which is hopeful for people who want to understand how women can act to change the world, rather than be victims of it. This kind of analysis is almost totally missing from any kind of women's history today. There are a few empirical studies but they tend not to generalise, and there are general studies which do not look at the changes that are taking place. The key question is how we can begin to bridge the gap by trying to develop a women's history which has respect for what has happened in the past, but also understands the kind of process we are living through, and therefore points the way to how we can change the future.

CHAPTER 4

Social history and the Russian Revolution

Mike Haynes

In this article I want to try to identify the main trends in the recent discussion of the Russian Revolution, to explain how these have come about and to restate the basic argument that it was circumstances rather than some totalitarian ideological drive that lay behind the initial degeneration of the revolution. This is a view which has come under sharp attack as, with the drift to the right in the late 1980s and early 1990s, historians of Russia have been influenced by the kind of critique of the left associated with the historian of the French Revolution, François Furet, who dismissed what he called 'the theory of circumstances' as being little more than an apologetic 'theory of extenuating circumstances'.[1]

From the 1960s writing on the Russian Revolution in the West increasingly reflected the work of 'social historians' writing 'history from below'. In the Russian case these historians attacked the Cold War idea that the revolution was a coup d'état manipulated (in the words of Leonard Schapiro) by a 'small, unpopular minority.' It was now argued that the revolution had genuine mass support from the workers of Russia (especially in Petrograd but also in Moscow), from the soldiers in the Red Army and, more ambiguously, from many peasants. These social groups came to support the Bolshevik Party in October as a result of the circumstances in which they found themselves making the seizure of power a genuine revolution rather than a coup d'état. The power of this argument was such that although it did not carry everything before it, it did nevertheless force earlier historians to reconsider their positions.[2]

Schapiro, for example, in the last book he wrote, recognised something of the force of this argument and, while insisting that the real issue was 'the inherent vice in Lenin's doctrine'—namely his and the Bolshevik's determination to hold on to power at all costs, he nevertheless included a element of personal memoir:

> In 1917, aged nine, I lived with my parents in Petrograd. We stayed there until late 1920. My family did not fall into the category of enemies of the regime, nor did they enjoy any priorities or privileges. Life was exceedingly hard. Diet was near starvation level, in the winter we suffered from freezing conditions for lack of fuel, breakdowns in public services were a normal occurrence. Stories of terror and brutality abounded. Yet my recollection, no doubt influenced by the adults around me, is one of enthusiasm and excitement. Life was new, hopeful, it was moving forward to some great future. In spite of the hardships and the brutality of the regime, the spirit of euphoria evoked by the fall of the monarchy in March 1917 was not yet dead.[3]

But while we must give full recognition to the importance of the work of this social history school and defend it against later attacks it is also important to realise that the works produced in this tradition often involved a number of serious deficiencies which prevented these historians from consistently developing their argument. An understanding of these weaknesses helps us to explain why, when this type of approach came under attack in the late 1980s and early 1990s, the response was muted and confusing if not one of more or less complete surrender.

The most important of these failures was the way in which social historians dealt with the issue of the relationship between their analysis of the revolution and its later degeneration into Stalinism. At first glance the analysis of 1917 as the triumph of popular democracy and initiative from below might seem to have re-enforced the argument that Stalinism was a compete betrayal of the revolution. Crushing the last remnants of independent initiative, Stalinism might have been thought to have shifted Russia completely off any revolutionary path by means of 'a revolution from above'. Unfortunately few historians went this far. These historians did not endorse Stalinism or its repression but they nevertheless tended to see it as an aberration on some socialist base. In the case of one group, associated in the United States with the historian Shelia Fitzpatrick, it almost seemed to be as if the argument was developing that if it could be shown that Stalinism had some popular support then this to some extent legitimised it.[4] Although this view was not widespread the general tone was informed by the kinds of political positions and historical judgements associated with Isaac Deutscher—that is an analysis of Stalinism weaker than that developed by Trotsky towards the end of his life and certainly not advancing towards the kind of attempt made by Tony Cliff to resolve the contradictions in Trotsky's argument by developing the view that the degeneration of the revolution led to a new form of state capitalism.[5]

Deutscher, and these later historians, too often instead retreated to the type of position associated with Trotsky and the left in the earlier stages of the degeneration in the 1920s and early 1930s. Then it was still believed that there was some possibility of halting the slide through internal bureaucratic reform. Perhaps, it was argued, there was still the possibility of reform by some benevolent bureaucratic grouping which would respond to the contradictions of the regime by opening it up.[6] There was thus both discontinuity and continuity at the same time since it appeared that by reform there could be some return to the earlier revolutionary phase. This inconsistent treatment of the continuity-discontinuity debate can be most clearly seen in one of the best known treatments of the problem by Stephen Cohen, the biographer of Bukharin. Cohen explicitly declared himself a discontinuity theorist, insisting that there were choices in the 1920s and that there was no totalitarian logic that drove the revolution to Stalin. But despite this he still appeared to accept that once the Stalin choice was made Russia remained in some sense socialist so that the force of his stress on discontinuity was dramatically reduced.[7]

This crucial inconsistency helps to explain how, when perestroika and glasnost began, many of these social historians fell over themselves to endorse in a barely qualified form the reform project of Mikhail Gorbachev. Now it appeared that a reforming wing of the bureaucracy was trying to restore some of the lost credibility of socialism. It is clear today that this was not the logic of the shift at all, instead the debates of the 1980s produced the conditions for the move to the market and private property in which there was an extensive conversion by the rulers of the former USSR of their 'state power' into 'private power'. The extent to which this has occurred now makes the judgements of only a few years ago look absurd. For instance, the leading economic historian R W Davies wrote in 1988 that 'in 1987 and 1988 we have seen nothing less than the rebirth of Soviet Marxism. The Marxist analysis of the Soviet experience is now one of the focal points of the whole debate.' Davies even allowed himself to speculate on what he called the 'alluring' prospect of 'a golden Soviet future.' Thus when the USSR collapsed these historians were inevitably disillusioned and tended to see the collapse not just as the death of Stalinism and its successors but as the end of a project that went back to, and in some sense derived directly from, 1917.[8]

A second problem relates to the analysis of 1917 itself. This has been the inability of 'history from below' to understand 1917 as class conflict. This might seem a strange thing to say in the light of the emphasis on working class in 1917 in these writings. But the problem is that class is a two sided relationship in which it is crucial to understand the imperatives that forced Russia's ruling class to act as it did. One historian, Diane Koenker in her book on Moscow workers, writes that in 1917 'capitalists began to behave as Marx said they would: no concessions to the workers, no compromises on the rights of factory owners'.[9] But if we look more carefully at the way in which this history was written then it is dismaying to find that often the capitalists are at best a ghostly presence. The ruling class history of 1917 was something that was left to more traditional historians. There is nothing wrong with history from below, *provided that it is informed by a good understanding of history from above* because class has to be about class conflict and class conflict always involves two sides. What these historians tended to do instead was write what we might call one legged history.[10]

The third problem with the social historians was that while their emphasis was ostensibly on class conflict they had a very crude understanding of working class politics. Essentially what they argued was that during 1917 the crisis that the working class experienced and, to a lesser extent, the crisis that the peasants experienced drove them to the left. But this pressure was very much materialistic—crudely it was something driven by the stomach rather than the head. The more hungry the workers, the more they clashed with their bosses and the state over issues like hours and wages and plant closures, the more bitter they became. Now this is obviously part of the process of radicalisation but it is not the whole process because this must involve the link between the stomach and the head in which political choices are made. Consider, for example, John Reed's famous description of workers coming out of the Putilov factory:

> What a marvellous sight to see the Putilovsky Zavod (the Putilov factory) pour out its forty thousands to listen to Social Democrats, Socialist revolutionaries, Anarchists, anybody, whatever they had to say, as long as they would talk! For months in Petrograd, and all over Russia, every street corner was a public tribune. In the railway trains, street-cars, always the spurting up of impromptu debate, everywhere.[11]

But in most of the accounts given by historians there is a more or less clear separation between the social and political dynamics of 1917. These historians appeared to be saying that floating above the class struggle is this thing called Bolshevik politics, which may or may not have been influenced by the events of 1917, but which is essentially an autonomous force created by Lenin, Trotsky and others. Below this is the popular movement starting at a low point in 1917 but then becoming more radical until it converges with Bolshevism in October 1917. Thus the revolution does have a popular base but this is a function of this convergence between two discrete elements. The same sociological dynamic that drives the workers up could then also drive them down again when social and economic problems multiplied, forcing workers to shut their doors on the world, so depoliticising them. Indeed this is an almost inevitable consequence of the argument given the separation between the social and political dynamics. A more adequate account of 1917 would have, therefore, to put the politics back into the social history of the revolution.[12]

However, in the late 1980s the possibility of a general development towards such an approach was derailed by a growing critique of the work of these historians from more hostile directions. Firstly the collapse of communism has led to the resurgence of a triumphalist right wing historiography reflected in works like Martin Malia's *The Soviet Tragedy. A History of Socialism in Russia, 1917-1991*, which is an attempt to rewrite the whole history of Russia since 1917 in term of a revitalised totalitarian approach and in the huge books on the Russian Revolution written by the American conservative historian Richard Pipes which have been called attempts at 'the prosecution of Soviet history'.[13] It is important to understand that this

61

type of approach has always been perhaps the most powerful current in Western discussion. One study of research on Russia in US universities notes that even at the high point of the social history school's influence only around 20 to 25 percent of PhD work on Russia fell into this area.[14] What is surprising is that so many social historians were so ill-prepared to meet this attack when it came.

From Russia too came disorientation as Stalinist history was stood on its head leading to a wholesale insistence on continuity and condemnation where once there had been continuity and praise. The work of Dmitri Volkogonov represents one reflection of this, easily available in the West. Volkogonov was the court historian of the perestroika-glasnost period beginning as a supporter of Gorbachev and writing a condemnatory biography of Stalin, then becoming nervous about the direction of events and turning to dismiss Trotsky. He ended his life, before cancer overwhelmed him, by supporting Yeltsin, rushing to finish a condemnatory biography of Lenin. Although Volkogonov is only one example of a modern Russian historian he is sufficiently representative in this respect to reflect the general thrust of mainstream history writing in Russia since the late 1980s.[15]

There was a third source of challenge from within social history from below. No less than elsewhere, historians of the Russian Revolution also began to be attracted to postmodernist approaches. Since the reasons for this are discussed elsewhere we will not rehearse them again here. Suffice it to say that the shift away from dealing with objective contradictions and rational responses played into the hands of those who for other reasons were hostile to the revolution.

We find therefore that a succession of former young Turks of the social history school advanced into the 1990s by throwing away many of their earlier views. Robert Service, for example, the author of a valuable study of the Bolshevik Party organisation, became professor of Russian history at the School of Slavonic Studies in London and the most visible face of this retreat flipping almost 180 degrees in his analysis.[16] In the United States, Ronald Grigor Suny also distanced himself from his earlier positions. Here was an excellent historian whose work graced the *New Left Review* as well as the finest historical journals, and who had published in 1983 a splendid discussion of the dynamics of the revolution under the title, 'Towards a Social History of the October

Revolution'. Now in response to Pipes he equivocated and took refuge in postmodernism.[17] Stephen Smith, the author of possibly the finest book on the working class in 1917, *Red Petrograd*, by 1994 was writing articles which declared that 'the system that was born in October 1917…can now be seen to have a beginning, a middle and an (uncertain!) end' so accepting a continuity thesis and like Suny, then offering a qualified postmodernist agenda as the way to redefine the debates on the revolution.[18] Neil Harding, whose books on Lenin's political thought represent two of the finest conventional attempts to understand Lenin's politics which he distilled with considerable sympathy, in his most recent book argues that Leninism 'replicated the dogmatic and intolerant themes of Marxism itself'.[19] Thus the attack turns not only on Lenin but from him to Marxism as something dogmatic and intolerant. In these and other cases the shift is so blatant that one must wonder how these historians explain the way in which they presented what must now appear as so many illusions in their earlier works. But this about turn finds its worst expression in the work of Orlando Figes, a poor imitation copy of Simon Schama's attack on the French Revolution in his *Citizens*.[20]

How do we explain this retreat? There is an obvious explanation that might appeal to historians. As a consequence of the collapse of the Soviet Union we are now able to identify from the archives evidence that tells us that our earlier views were wrong. No serious historian would dismiss the importance of archival work but when we look at the experience of a country like Russia the argument that the secrets are in the archives is grossly misleading. Was it really the case that we had to go to the archives to understand the nature of Soviet society and especially what was wrong with that society? The answer is of course, no. In the West it was perfectly possible to see and analyse what was wrong with that society. Of course we could not dot every *i* or cross every *t* but the basic shape of the story was clear from afar— indeed perhaps clearer. We did not need the collapse of 1991 to tell us that here was a society based on oppression and exploitation, a society of illusions.

But what is perhaps striking in the first instance is the disappointing nature of the evidence produced by the archives. Much time has been invested both in popular and academic discussion to 'dish the dirt' on Lenin but with little effect it seems because there is no significant dirt to dish. A 1997 BBC documentary, for example, for which Robert Service acted as the historical adviser, could only find three points of attack—Lenin had supported terror against the rich peasants during the civil war, he may have had an affair with Inessa Armand and, most astonishing of all, it was claimed that Lenin had pushed forward the revolution because of his fear of an early death![21] One might imagine that 'academic works' offered more substantive new evidence, but a glance at *The Unknown Lenin: From the Secret Archive* edited by Richard Pipes will quickly disabuse the reader that this is so as the most trivial documents are presented as new evidence combined with a commentary by Pipes that reveals the most astonishingly tendentious (mis)interpretation of the documents.[22]

Indeed—to play devil's advocate—if we want to make the argument that what is at stake is the archival evidence and this should force us to change our minds, then the single most important archival revelation might ironically lead to a more benign view of Stalinism rather than a more hostile one. This is because the archives appear to have shown the numbers of people who died under Stalinism and the numbers of people arrested, though enormous, were substantially less than we imagined. Since the historians who had equivocated on Stalinism had by and large accepted the higher figures then logically if the historiographical shift were driven by evidence alone this should lead to a more positive attitude to Soviet history. Thus whereas Robert Conquest, the leading expert on these problems in the West had argued that there were a minimum of 17 million excess deaths between 1930 and 1938 from famine, purges and executions it now appears that there were actually nearer 10 million; and whereas he argued that there was a prison camp population of 9 million in 1938 it appears now that this figure, for all those in prison, camps, colonies and special settlements, reached a pre-war peak of 3.35 million in 1941 and a post-war peak of 5.5 million in 1953. Finally, whereas the number of executions had been thought to run into millions it now appears that between 1921 and 1952 there were some 800,000, 85 percent of which were carried out in 1937 to 1938 alone.[23]

Thus the substantive dimensions of the terror appear to have been significantly less than was imagined. Let me stress it is not my argument that this should change our view of Stalinism. The point is that if the issue were 'archival evidence', then given the earlier assumptions common to so many social historians, the debate might have gone in a completely different direction. These historians knew of Conquest's work, largely accepted his estimates, and still found something positive in the USSR. Indeed, when the outcome of perestroika was still unclear to some commentators, we can find historians worrying about exactly these implications of what one critic of social history called 'extreme archival fetishism'.[24]

Thus it clearly cannot be the archives that has caused this shift in views. Rather history is reflecting present politics and the weaknesses of the social history school therefore reflects their own hesitations and ambiguities read back into their historical work. Some will no doubt consider this accusation unfair and crude but the power of the present to remould our understanding of the past and the way in which the past is twisted to support the present can be seen especially clearly in the way in which commentators in Russia have approached Russian history since 1985-86.

Part of the task of historians since that date has been that of historical excavation to reveal a less mythologised picture of the past. Discussions of Russian history have usually concentrated on this entirely healthy process. But other influences have also been at work. During the transition to post-Francoist Spain, for example, a similar process of excavation took place to reveal a history submerged by Francoist ideas. But the history that resulted also involved arguments about the present and the form that the transition should take. Just as discussion of the past opened up some themes, so others were half consciously closed off, squeezing out radical interpretations of the Spanish past that might legitimate a more fundamental transition. Exactly the same process can be seen in the themes of many in Russia who comment on Russian history—history has become part of the debate over the transition, part of the attempt to set limits and to construct a narrow view of the transition.

Firstly, let us take the emphasis on totalitarianism. The theory of 'totalitarianism' has a long history and has been subjected to powerful critiques in the West. Moshe Lewin famously attacked totalitarianism as 'useless as a conceptual category...the term was...itself "totalitarian" in its empty self sufficiency; it did not recognise any mechanism of change in the Soviet Union and had no use for even a shadow of some historical process'.[25] Why then has it proved so popular in Russia? The answer does not lie in the intellectual merits of the argument so much as the way in which the use of the idea of totalitarianism creates an aura of radicalism for its proponents and enables them to shuffle off their own responsibility for the past by arguing that they were all victims of a powerful system that could not be resisted.

Consider, for example, the position of Dmitri Volkogonov, who tried to endear himself to his readers by confessing his own agonising reappraisal of the past when he described how 'it is hard to write this as a former Stalinist who has made the painful transition to a total rejection of Bolshevik totalitarianism, I confess that Leninism was the last bastion to fall in my mind.' But Volkogonov was a Soviet general who, before he became associated with Gorbachev's reforms, established his position in military education through his expertise in what was called 'military-patriotic education' and 'the struggle against the ideological diversions of imperialism'. In this way he was able to rise to become director of the Institute of Military History and deputy director of the Central Political Directorate of the Soviet army, as well as essentially the court historian of Gorbachev and Yeltsin. Or take Alexander Yakolev, who rose to become a key intellectual proponent of perestroika, writing later that the Soviet Union was a 'hideous system of statism, bureaucratic absolutism, economic ruin, and spiritual suppression of the individual, it was a society based on violence and fear.' He too was no less anxious to engage the reader's sympathy with his own plight: 'it is painful to know that you have been dominated for many decades by myths, not by common sense.' But was it so difficult under the old system to know this? Were there not dissidents who paid for knowing this with imprisonment? Should not these highly placed people have known, and is there not truth in the accusation that their enthusiasm for the concept of totalitarianism is little more than a self serving ideological escape route?

But the problem extends beyond this to the mechanics of history writing. Volkogonov expressed a suspicion of ordinary Russians that is sadly all too typical of many commentators. At one point he even manages to load a significant part of the responsibility for Stalinism on the shoulders of the working class, arguing that workers 'involuntarily delegated [their] power to a tenacious, imperious and all-seeing stratum of professional Leninist Party members... The working class thus served as the most important mass instrument for the forced introduction of socialism in Russia'.[26] This type of approach has a double effect. Firstly, it feeds the *amour propre* of the Russian intelligentsia, what even appears as their intellectual snootiness, as they disdainfully try to draw a line between themselves and 'their suffering' and the lower orders in a way sometimes reminiscent of the lower middle class in Britain before 1914.[27] Secondly, it helps to feed the argument that in terms of the transition it does not matter if even a minimal democratic input from those at the bottom of Russian society is discounted because it may be too dangerous to pay more attention to their interests, as the reformer Grigory Yavlinsky put it, 'the idea of social justice is one of the most dangerous political ideas there has been. It has been proved over and over again that the struggle for social justice ends horrifically'.[28]

Behind this lies a general discrediting of historical alternatives which underpins the view that only one form of exit from Stalinism was possible. It is not surprising then to find that history written in this way can be held together with the crudest of assumptions about the nature of society. Thus Yakolev now tells us that 'private property, the market, and democracy are the genetic code of normal civilisation'.[29]

The irony is, of course, that this has led to programmes of transition which in their mindless pursuit of market solutions resemble nothing so much as Stalin's pursuit of the 'plan'. This market Stalinism has been carried through with enormous costs. Alec Nove once described what happened in Russia in the revolution from above: 'The fact still seems to be clear: 1933 was the culmination of the most precipitous peacetime decline in living standards known in recorded history'.[30] It also brought, of course, the Soviet famine of 1933—a 'policy made' disaster usually laid at the feet of Stalin and his supporters. Yet now the shift back to the market has involved just as dramatic an attack on the living standards of the descendants of the generations that suffered in Russia in the 1930s and, if anything, the precipitous decline in living standards of 1991-1995 has outdone that of 1929-1933 in Russia.

This simple fact ought to give pause for thought to those who argue for continuity between 1917 and 1991. If there is continuity in Russian history does it not lie in the way in which those who were victorious in 1928-1932, and their successors, were able to maintain their rule across the divide of 1991? The individuals at

the top are well known—Boris Yeltsin—from Communist appa-
ratchik to president; Viktor Chernomyrdin—from 'red director'
to multi-millionaire and prime minister. But beneath them is a
whole ruling class shifting its power from its control of state capital to new combinations of control of state and private capital.[31]

The real discontinuity might then appear between 1917 and
1928-32. It was the revolution from above in the period of the
first five year plan that created the basis for the power of these
groups. But to sustain this argument we need to explain how the
revolution degenerated to a situation where a new ruling class
could come to power. We cannot here detail the history of the
struggles in the 1920s that eventually led to this outcome, readers can find this story elsewhere.[32] But we can restate the basic
argument about the way in which degeneration emerged from the
material contradictions of the time and apply it to the first stages
of collapse in the civil war years.

This argument was well summed up by Peter Sedgwick: 'The
"objective" social circumstances of Russia's revolution and civil
war contain sufficient conditions for the collapse of the mass revolutionary wave, without recourse to causal factors stemming
from the "subjective" deficiencies of Lenin's early formulations'.[33] The crucial thing to understand about the Russian
Revolution after 1917 is the way in which the revolutionaries
suddenly found themselves in a spiral of decline and decay over
which they had little control thus dramatically restricting the kind
of choices that could be made. Alternatives were not plucked out
of the air or simply informed by ideological disagreements, they
were brutally determined by the crisis that people faced.

If we look at what we can call 'the structure of choice' within
which decisions were made then we can see that this was becoming progressively narrower as the civil war proceeded and society
was affected by social collapse as revolutionary Russia became a
'beleaguered fortress'. The scale of this collapse bears comparison with the great social disasters of the 20th century. Table 1
opposite shows the collapse in key urban centres. For those who
remained in the towns even the basic infrastructure collapsed as
deprived of fuel, urban services seized up and the winter cold
burst the sewage and water systems.

Taking the 1914 figure as the point of comparison understates
the fall for some towns which benefited from war time expansion.
Petrograd, for example, had an average population of 2.3 million

in 1917 and perhaps 2.4 million before numbers began to slide, while in Moscow the population in September 1917 was 1.854 million. As can be seen from the table, however, the population slumped in most towns save those in the south which became bloated refugee centres. In general a glance at the map will show that the biggest falls were in those towns in what was known as the grain consuming areas of the country where urban life depended on food travelling north in return for industrial goods travelling south.

Table 1: Changes in the population of the leading towns 1897-1920[34]

	1897	1914	1920	% change 1914-20
St Petersburg	1,264,900	2,118,500	722,000	-66
Moscow	1,038,600	1,762,700	1,028,000	-42
Odessa	403,800	499,600	435,000	-13
Kiev	247,700	520,500	366,000	-30
Kharkov	174,000	244,700	284,000	+16
Saratov	137,100	235,700	190,000	-19
Ekaterinoslav	112,800	211,100	164,000	-22
Tiflis	159,600	307,300	327,000	+6
Kazan	130,000	194,200	146,000	-25
Baku	119,900	232,200	256,000	+10
Astrakhan	112,900	151,500	123,000	-19
Rostov-on-Don	119,500	172,300	177,000	+3
Nizhny Novgorod	90,100	111,600	70,000	-37
Ufa	49,300	99,900	93,000	-6
Minsk	90,700	116,700	104,000	-11
Samara	90,000	143,800	177,000	+23
Tsaritisyn	55,200	100,800	81,000	-20
Perm	45,200	68,100	74,000	+9

Conditions in the towns were set by the simple threat of starvation. This can be clearly seen in the debate on food requisitioning where it is often argued that if only the Bolsheviks had pursued a softer line against the peasantry then life would have been easier. Post-revolutionary policy certainly faltered in terms of trying to encourage the poor peasants to rise against the middle peasants as Lenin himself realised in late 1918. But the fundamental problem was that nothing was being produced to encourage the peasants to exchange for grain. The beginnings of food requisitioning in fact pre-date October as the supply system

69

began to collapse. Post-October policy involved a clear recognition that if an exchange between the countryside and the town was to take place then the town have to produce goods for the peasants. One consequence of this was the attempt in the winter of 1917-18 to convert a number of military plants to civilian production but these attempts failed as supplies of all kinds dried up and the losses of the Brest-Litovsk Treaty were reinforced by the development of the civil war. The extent of the goods shortage is well documented in contemporary accounts as is the frustration of the peasants with money that lost its value.

Lacking the most basic goods to exchange, and in the context of war, it is difficult to see what choice the Bolsheviks had other than grain requisition, however much that may have provoked peasant hostility. As one contemporary put it, 'What do you think, the People's Commissariat of Food Supply does this for its own satisfaction? No. We do it because there's not enough food.' Tsiurupa, from the Commissariat of Food Supplies, put the choice bluntly: 'There are only two possibilities: either we perish from hunger, or we weaken the [peasant] economy to some extent, but [manage] to get out of our temporary difficulties'.[35]

But the collapse went far beyond this as society regressed backwards to an almost unimaginable degree. Horrific waves of epidemic disease swept across Russia. Typhus, spread by lice, was one of the most feared. At this time Russia experienced what has been called 'the greatest typhus epidemic in history'. Officially there were some 7 million cases but the real figure was perhaps double this with a 10 percent death rate. The Red Army alone experienced some 550,000 to 600,000 cases resulting in perhaps 100,000 deaths. Such terrible conditions seemed to set at nothing the earlier bold hopes, reducing politics not only to a grim battle to survive against the counter-revolution without, but also against the forces of chaos within. As Lenin put it in 1919, 'either lice will conquer socialism or socialism will conquer the lice.' Disinfectant teams in Moscow, for example, were treating 40,000 to 50,000 people a day at railway stations to delouse them. It was said that at one delousing room at the end of the day the lice lay two inches thick on the floor.[36]

Table 2 opposite shows how the numbers of industrial workers changed as this crisis developed. Here the arguments that the Bolsheviks, having come to power with the support of the working class, then lost their class base as the working class turned against them, foundered on the fact that only a distorted rump of workers remained in the key towns. Column 1 shows the numbers of workers from which the terrible scale of the collapse is apparent enough. But these figures relate to the whole of Russia. During the civil war many areas slipped from Bolshevik control. Fairly precise estimates could be made of the number of workers who remained in areas under Bolshevik control but we do not have them. Column 2 therefore shows a cruder estimate of the numbers in the 24 provinces of European Russia that formed the core area of Bolshevik territory when the revolutionary regime was at its weakest. Column 3 brings these two elements together to give a rough idea of the changing numbers of workers under Bolshevik control as the front changed and the social collapse developed. The figure for August 1918 represents the census figure of workers in 32 provinces of European Russia and excludes enemy territory and territory too close to fighting for the census to be taken. The figure for 1919 represents the column 2 figure and that for 1920 and 1921 the figures after the military consolidation of the revolution. For all its crudeness this table hopefully brings out the central point that at the worst time in the civil war the working class base of the regime had been

Table 2: Estimates of the size of the industrial working class in Russia 1913-1922[37]

	Russia	Index	24 provinces in European Russia	Area under Bolshevik control	Index
1913	3,100,000	86			
1917	3,600,000	100	1,850,000	3,600,000	100
1918	2,500,000	69	1,071,000	1,150,000	32
1919	1,400,000	39			
1919*			910,000	910,000	25
1919**			760,000	760,000	21
1920	1,500,000	42	735,000	1,500,000	42
1921	1,200,000	33		1,200,000	31
1922	1,100,000	31		1,100,000	31

* average first half
**average second half

ripped apart in a way that even some of the best accounts of the time underestimate. Workers' power, however much we might wish it, could not exist in this situation. The soviets collapsed as living forces and power inevitably gravitated upwards and the party leadership became fused with the former institutions of popular power.

The best workers joined the Red Army or worked in the new revolutionary state, often in new areas. Workers left the cities in their hundreds of thousands to find salvation in the countryside. Even skilled workers took this way out of the starving cities not simply because they might have families in the rural areas but because they might be able to turn their skills to local needs—perhaps a starving skilled or semi-skilled metal worker might hope to eke out a living, even without land, by repairing ploughs, implements and pots and pans. The ranks of those that stayed behind were then further reduced by disease and early death in the extreme conditions of the day.

Petrograd offers an extreme case of how these pressures affected the basic institutions of political power. The soviet in the city continued to be re-elected every six months but the number of deputies was allowed to exceed the theoretical constitutional maximum because of the instability of the membership. Even within the electoral periods the Red Army component was, of course, subject to regular change as soldiers went off elsewhere. But so too was the civilian component as deputies were expected to show the lead in response to the mobilisations of the time. Thus in December 1918, 14 out of the 29 executive members of the soviet were reported to have joined the Red Army. The overall losses to the soviet from different sources were documented for the period January to June 1920 (after the period of greatest turmoil). Of the 1,924 deputies, 118 deputies were directed to work in other parts of the country; 63 were mobilised for the front; 18 left because of illness; six died; 56 were excluded for infractions of party discipline; 20 were recalled by their electors; seven were removed because of abuse of power and criminal activity; two refused to work in the soviet and 21 left Petrograd of their own accord. The constant turnover of membership against the background of social collapse and the collapse of the working class led to the centre of gravity of the soviet being swung not only away from the workplace but also from the ordinary deputies. Although the biggest group of deputies were workers by 'social origin' the number of deputies who were working in the factory declined continuously until in the second half of 1920, 51.1 percent of deputies were on social, party, economic, soviet, military or trade union work; 19.9 percent were from the Red Army in one form or another; and only 26.6 percent worked in various work places (2.4 percent were housewives). Moreover, inevitably in this crisis atmosphere, the deputies who came from the factories were not necessarily themselves still 'workers at the bench' as they had been in 1917 since such militants now made up the thin layer of working class leaders in factory management.[38]

Trotsky had once famously predicted that what he then (mis)understood as Leninism might lead to substitutionism where 'the party organisation [the caucus] at first substitutes itself for the party as a whole; then the Central Committee substitutes itself for the organisation; and finally a single "dictator" substitutes himself for the Central Committee'. Though Trotsky later rejected this view of Lenin's theory of the party, the idea fits neatly with those who see the problem as essentially an ideological one and ever since then has been held up as a prescient criticism of Bolshevism. Here, however, we see that substitutionism reflected real material processes rather than an immanent logic of idea or organisation. Material pressures were so powerful that ideas and organisation could not resist them and therefore became inevitably influenced by them rather than vice versa. In abstract we therefore might agree with the left Socialist Revolutionary, Spiridonova, that 'the Soviets must be like a sensitive barometer connected to the people; therefore unconditional freedom of election, the free play of the spontaneous will must prevail; only then will creative energy, a new life, a living organism come into being'.[39] But this made no sense in the midst of the civil war and the loss of the working class base not just for the soviets but for the wider political debate. At the end of the civil war the Worker's Opposition would encounter the same dilemma. It is difficult for any socialist not to sympathise with the arguments of Kollontai and Shliapnikov but realism also dictates that we recognise just how precarious the base of the regime was and just how unrealistic it was to demand power for a working class which no longer existed. Trotsky had gone on in his early discussion of substitutionism to suggest that 'the party must seek the guarantee of its stability in its own base, in an active and self reliant proletariat, and not in its top caucus, which the revolution...may suddenly sweep away.'

But it was exactly this base of stability, an active self reliant proletariat that had been destroyed.[40]

The dilemma was recognised at the time and it is quite wrong to imagine that there was an easy solution. The processes of collapse were just as evident in the provinces and this was why, in 1919, the Democratic Centralist opposition *within* the Bolshevik Party argued for increased party control of the Soviets just because of their fears that they were becoming less and less representative. But the party itself could not escape these pressures too.[41] We can see this in Petrograd. If we examine the composition of the Bolshevik group in the Petrograd soviet in January-June 1920, we find that only 99 had joined the party before 1917, 220 in 1917 and 790 between 1918 and 1920, with 300 not giving information (and, since there was such pride attached to membership during and before 1917, likely therefore to be post 1917 members). Thus even in Petrograd by 1920 at least 56 percent of Bolshevik deputies and probably nearer 75 percent had joined the party *after* the revolution. It would be wrong to completely dismiss the motives of those who joined during the civil war. As Lenin said at this time, 'a party membership ticket under these circumstances meant something approaching a candidature for Denikin's gallows'. But equally the element of opportunism, careerism and the problem of the quality of the recruits cannot be ignored, especially as the best new members were almost immediately sent off to hold the line somewhere else so that the party's numbers in a town like Petrograd reflected a turnover within its ranks. One estimate suggests that between July 1918 and the end of 1920 some 20,000 party members, candidates and supporters in Petrograd were mobilised and probably left the city. Here we see the material base of the contrast between the mass of deputies and the executive of the soviet where 43 percent of Bolsheviks had a pre-1917 membership and a further 16 percent had joined in 1917.[42]

The contradictions that this created are well brought out in the contemporary writings of Victor Serge, some of which are collected in *Revolution in Danger*. What Serge does is to explain the reality of these narrowing choices as they were lived by people in the civil war. Here we find a celebration and defence of the libertarian vision of the revolution even as its leadership was forced to tread much of it under foot in order just to survive and to try to preserve the rest. Trying to explain this to his anarchist friends

Serge, perhaps more than any other writer, allows us to appreciate just how difficult were the material circumstances and political choices.[43]

As these circumstances changed, and society with them, so ideology began to reflect this. But to understand this we have to sensitively tease out changing ideas. Here ironically those historians who stress Leninism as an ideological force are ill-equipped to help because they simply do not pay attention to the ideas that they claim are so important. This is well brought out in a powerful critique by Lars Lih of the way in which a classic work of the civil war period has been treated, *The ABC of Communism* by Bukharin and Preobrazhensky. Lih details how this book has been used to show the power of ideas and the way in which a key section of the Bolsheviks wanted to drive forward to a leap to communism, seeing in the chaos of war communism the birth of new socialist forms. But Lih tellingly demonstrates how this represents almost exactly the opposite of what the text says and it can only be maintained if Bukharin and Preobrazhensky's actual argument, which emphasises the problems of the time, is ignored. Lih's argument not only undermines the ideological continuity thesis but also raises fundamental questions about the professional standards of the historians who hold to it.[44] Here is a surreal world where historians who cannot be bothered to read the texts and situate them, pride themselves on the fact that their superiority as historians lies in the seriousness with which they understand ideas, language and context!

But the argument about circumstances also applies no less to the counter-revolution. If the options for the Bolsheviks were narrowed, so too were those of their opponents, revealing class choices from the other side. This too is obscured by many accounts which take a benign view of the counter-revolution even as they condemn the Bolsheviks. Yet the record of the Whites demonstrates a level of violence, brutality and cynicism on an astonishing scale. Their determination to restore a regime based on private property drove this brutality forward. Material pressures could at times equal those in the Bolshevik areas. In Rostov, in the south, one British officer recorded the situation at Christmas 1919:

> There was no fuel to thaw water or heat it for a bath, or to wash clothes in: water pipes had frozen and burst; few people possessed spare shirts or underclothes: as for avoiding crowds, you could not

move a step without running the risk of infection. The railway stations and trains were the worst typhus traps.[45]

White armies came into the countryside looking for support, food, Bolsheviks and Jews. General Krasnov addressed himself to the peasants, calling on them to harvest the corn of several thousand acres. He promised them protection and gratitude. 'The appeal has had no success; the corn remains in the fields', wrote one contemporary. It is easy to understand why when the fear that the peasants had that the land would be returned to the landowners was compounded by leaflets like the following:

> Today my aeroplanes will throw these leaflets; tomorrow think a while; the day after send away the robbers; send them by the Volga, the way they came; throw away your arms. When the bells toll, come over to your brothers, the Cossacks, and we will all pray together in your holy churches. Then trains will run to the Caucuses, to the west, to the Ukraine, and you will get everything you need. But if you resist, take warning. Woe to you! I arrive with 200,000 men, picked troops, hundreds and hundreds of cannon. I bring 3,000 balloons of asphyxiating gas; I shall asphyxiate the whole country. It will be death to all who live.[46]

Krasnov was not alone. On the north western front an evocative description of Yudenich was left by one of his senior officers, Colonel Boris P Poliakov, 'Here the Whites also faced shortages of clothing, shoes, equipment and food which they had to solve by imposing duties, buying and selling and the issue of treasury bills. Yudenich had 1,500 million roubles printed which it was claimed would exchange at 40 to the pound when Petrograd was taken.' Poliakov writes that 'the civilian population and the armed forces personnel received paper money with a very dubious purchasing power, and on the other hand, the government and the commander in chief who promoted this money widely, were looked upon as people carrying out some kind of swindle.' Yudenich's army developed an overblown bureaucracy with at one stage 56 generals and 4,650 officers of whom only 600 were at the front. 'In Narva still exist coffee houses with quite good orchestras', wrote a journalist, 'where people can sit in British uniforms, whistling pleasantly and concocting new plans for the seizure of Petrograd. But beyond the coffee houses the army was reduced to human shadows roaming around with vacant faces'.[47]

If the Bolsheviks were victims of circumstances in this crucial period this does not mean that the civil war fell out of the sky on them. It could only happen on the scale that it did because of the support of the counter-revolution by the West. The commitment of men and resources and moral authority to the Whites was something that the West could afford to undertake at relatively little cost to itself. But its effect in Russia was devastating given the weakness and backwardness of society. Without this Western aid it is probable that White opposition would not have developed to anything like the same extent and certain it would have faltered more quickly. There was thus a basic asymmetry in power relations which has been all too sadly characteristic of Western intervention in more backward countries this century. What appears in the core of capitalism as low cost action wreaks havoc on the vulnerable parts of the world.

Here again much contemporary historical writing falters because it offers an essentially benign approach to Western intervention. This approach not only minimises its impact but underplays its rationale. Some historians have gone to the extreme of arguing that the problem with Western intervention was that it did not go far enough and the West should have used more resources to destroy the Bolsheviks. But the most common argument takes almost the opposite point of view seeing intervention as an unfortunate accident. The initial aim in 1918 was dictated by war interests but, once intervention was begun, the Western powers found themselves sucked into an anti-Bolshevik crusade from which the best politicians then struggled to escape.

In opposition to this we do not need to produce a vast conspiracy theory although sections of the establishment were certainly plotting at this time to keep up the pressure for intervention. What we do have to do is to look at the way in which the structural imperatives of the need to stabilise post-war capitalism initially led to the intervention and then conditioned and limited it.

This leads to another crucial explanatory factor. Western intervention was only able to have the effect it did because the revolution did not spread to the West as the Bolsheviks hoped and expected and because too little opposition was developed by western socialists to the actions of their own governments in Russia. Yet many historians on the left now follow traditional right wing and liberal history condemning 'the myth of the international revolution', though it is interesting to find the arch-conservative

Richard Pipes attacking Figes for his failure to take this argument sufficiently seriously.[48] When historians disparage the opportunity for change that existed beyond Russia's borders in 1918-21 the argument about the Russian Revolution comes full circle. Now the narrowing of historical options is not just a matter of writing about the Russian Revolution in particular but history in general. The delegitimisation of the Russian Revolution leads into an argument that lifts the burden of guilt from the inadequacies of Western socialism. Yesterday's enemies become today's realists, rejecting 'utopian advance'. What was possible was essentially what happened. How strange that this is where we should end up for many of the historians who would now happily argue this position once identified with E P Thompson's famous call to 'lift the tremendous condescension of the present' from those who struggled in the past. Now it would appear that we are expected to glorify in the condescension of the present as real historical turning points are dismissed and the actions of those who see different possibilities become of no more relevance to us than old time sects.

But if we are to resist this, and the whole argument here is that we should, we have one more piece of the puzzle to add. In 1920-21 the Bolsheviks succeeded in winning the civil war in Russia. The cost of the civil war and the related social dislocation was enormous in terms of lives lost and destruction. Worse still the revolution was now isolated. Yet once the war had ended and the shock of Kronstadt, the Tambov Revolt and the New Economic Policy had been felt, was there not still an opportunity in this situation to begin, at least in small ways, to restore some of the lost democracy of 1917? Yet within a couple of years the degeneration had taken hold to a fantastically greater degree —why? Part of the answer can be seen in Table 2 on page 71 which extends the data for the decline of the working class to 1922. What is not often enough appreciated is that the recovery of Russian society in general and the working class in particular did not really begin until the late summer of 1922. The months between the ending of the civil war and the onset of recovery in August-September 1922 were dominated by a new and fearsome struggle against one of the great famines of the 20th century in the Volga which may have killed as many as five million people. 'As a result of the continued and growing food crisis we are compelled to characterise the state of all branches of our national economy as being on the brink of disaster. This is not a phrase, but bitter reality,' said *Pravda* on 16 July 1921. The scale of this new peacetime crisis was so great that many of the methods of 'war communism' were carried over into the new society of the New Economic Policy where, combining with new social dynamics, they helped to solidify what had been wartime reactions to circumstances into new patterns of behaviour and rule that were now taken for granted and associated with 'Bolshevik ways'. Critics of the Bolsheviks were only too happy to lay the blame for the famine at the door of the revolution.

We might see a more complex chain of causes as did close observers at the time. A mass of documentation exists from charity workers who went to Russia to help out which describes the horror of this period. But the very fact that this documentation comes from charity workers tells us something else. Despite the aspirations to humanitarianism the official society of the West stood by while the horror unfolded—a pattern that has since become all too familiar. The biggest single source of aid to the starving came from the American Relief Administration—indirectly assisted by the US government—but European governments, despite fine words, left it by and large to private agencies. As the news of the scale of the suffering begin to filter through to Western Europe, Lloyd George, speaking to the Supreme Allied Council in Paris in early August 1921, appeared to offer the promise of substantial assistance, 'When a house is burning down you do not ask questions about the owner. You make efforts to save it'.[49] But it was just these 'questions about the owner' which stymied even basic assistance.

As it did so the Russian leadership was pulled even more to look in on itself and a further stage of the degeneration of the revolution towards socialism in one country was laid. In May 1922 we find Kalinin, speaking to the All-Russian Central Executive Committee of the Soviets, saying, 'As a whole the famine relief effort made by the Russian working class has been magnificent. One cannot help comparing it, a little bitterly, with the relatively insignificant help afforded by the West European working class movement'.[50] When German socialists in 1923 failed to take advantage of the revolutionary situation in that year the commitment of a central part of the leadership, now under pressure from the bureaucracy around it, finally swung round towards a more explicit abandonment of the internationalism of the original revolution. In the next

79

years the different oppositions would try to halt this slide until they too would be swept away along with the remaining gains of the revolution after 1928. The wheel would have turned full circle and the revolution was lost even though the new regime still tried to cloak itself with its own distorted myth of its revolutionary origins. That regime has now thankfully fallen too, at least in its political form. But this is all the more reason to defend the real history of the revolution and its degeneration and to save it from those historians who would distort and bury it no less effectively than did the supporters of Stalin and his successors, so obscuring the past in the name of the present and the present in the name of the past.

CHAPTER 5

Labour and the English Revolution

Brian Manning

Marx and Engels held that exploitation of labour and conflict of classes were the fundamental factors in history from the earliest times to the present. As they said in *The Communist Manifesto*, 'The history of all past society has consisted in the development of class antagonisms, antagonisms that assumed different forms at different epochs. But whatever form they may have taken, one fact is common to all past ages, viz the exploitation of one part of society by the other.' 'The whole history of mankind...has been a history of class struggles, contests between exploiting and exploited, ruling and oppressed classes... Freeman and slave, patrician and plebeian, lord and serf, guildmaster and journeyman, in a word oppressor and oppressed'.[1] Not every conflict between groups in society springs from class antagonism, but when two groups stand in a relation of exploiters and exploited, it is a class relation; and when one group seeks to exploit another group, and the latter group strives to ward off exploitation, they become engaged in class struggle.[2]

In volume one of *Capital* Marx defined exploitation in terms of 'necessary' and 'surplus' labour: necessary labour was that part of labour required for the subsistence of the producer and surplus labour was that part of labour appropriated from the producer by the exploiter. 'Surplus labour was not a new discovery made by capital', he wrote: it existed in ancient Greece and Rome; it was appropriated by Norman barons and American slave owners, as well as by modern landowners and capitalists.

81

He drew a parallel between the medieval peasant and the modern factory worker. 'Let us suppose', he said, 'that the working day comprises six hours of necessary labour and six hours of surplus labour. Then the free worker gives the capitalist every week 36 hours of surplus labour. It is just as if he were to work three days a week on his own account and three days a week gratuitously for the capitalist.' The unfree serf owed labour services to his lord and worked, say, three days a week on his own plot of ground and three days a week on his lord's land. 'Three days of surplus labour in a week', concluded Marx, 'remain three days of labour for which the worker receives no equivalent; and it does not matter whether we call them' labour services of the medieval peasant or the wage labour of the modern factory worker.[3] Of course Marx did distinguish between the feudal mode of production and the capitalist mode of production (in this example the peasant possesses the means of production and the factory worker does not) but the point he was making was that both modes exploit labour.

Maurice Dobb wrote that 'basically the mode of production under feudalism was the petty mode of production': production by peasants and artisans who possessed the means of production. Part of their product was extracted from them to support the feudal ruling class, and so 'the crucial class struggle under feudalism' was between the small producers and the feudal lords.[4] This remained the case during the transition from feudalism to capitalism, except that in addition to exploitation by feudal lords, small producers were exploited by emerging capitalists. In a bourgeois revolution both the aristocracy and the bourgeoisie are exploiting classes and, as Boris Porchnev pointed out, concentration on those two classes may lead to missing or effacing the conflict between exploiters and exploited, which he called 'the really fundamental antagonism between classes'.[5]

A crucial distinction, however, is between small producers who possessed the means of production and had part of the product of their labour transferred to landlords and merchants, and wage labourers who did not possess the means of production but had only their labour power, which they exchanged for wages. There were wage labourers under feudalism as well as under capitalism, but the transition from feudalism to capitalism involved the transference of wage labour from exploitation by feudal lords to exploitation by capitalist employers. Small producers and wage labourers formed the labour force of pre-industrial society. Small producers as well as wage labourers earned their livings by long hours of hard manual labour, and the basic distinction of status in traditional society was between the lower strata who gained their livelihood by working with their hands and the upper strata who received their livelihood without having to engage in manual labour.[6] However, small producers were also employers of labour and therefore were themselves exploiters, as well as being exploited by feudal lords and merchants.

Norah Carlin has raised the question of the role of wage workers in the English Revolution.[7] The purpose of my essay is to consider how far the wage labourers had been drawn into the capitalist mode of production and so become a proletariat, at the time of the English Revolution, and how far small producers had developed into capitalists and so become a bourgeoisie; and the emerging class differences which shaped the course and outcome of the revolution.

The extent and limits of proletarianisation

Capitalism and a market economy was developing in 17th century England, involving increasing production for the market by means of employing more wage labour. Engels provided a framework for investigation:

> From its origin the bourgeoisie was saddled with its antithesis: capitalists cannot exist without wage workers, and, in the same proportion as the medieval burgher of the guild developed into the modern bourgeois, so the guild journeyman and the day labourer outside the guilds developed into the proletarian.

And he went on to say that 'in every great bourgeois movement there were independent outbursts of that class which was the more or less developed forerunner of the modern proletariat'.[8]

Under the tradition of craft production in manufacture the craftsman or artisan, organised in the guilds and companies, served an apprenticeship and then worked as a wage earning journeyman until he could accumulate the resources to rent a workshop, purchase tools and raw materials, and set up his own business as a small master, himself often employing an apprentice or two and a journeyman. In the 16th century it was 'a reasonable expectation' for most journeymen after a few years to establish themselves as independent small producers with their own workshops, and in fact about four fifths did so, although it took longer for some than others.[9] This may have continued to be the case down to the revolution of the 17th century, for Norah Carlin argues that the career prospect of journeymen in London companies may not have deteriorated until after the Restoration, and Eric Kerridge maintains that in textile manufactures it was unlikely that most of the journeymen 'remained employees all their working lives'.[10] Nevertheless, at the time of the revolution many apprentices and journeymen in London were experiencing anxiety about whether they would be able to set up in business for themselves.[11] And in a study of London after the Restoration, Tim Harris accepts that 'a class of permanent journeymen had…come into existence, men who had neither the capital nor the opportunity to set up an independent business of their own', but continued to work as wage earners.[12]

Whether or not growing numbers of journeymen remained wage earners all their lives, a general increase in the numbers of wage workers may be posited for areas of agriculture and manufacture falling under capitalist control. Alan Everitt has spoken of the emergence in agriculture before the revolution of '…a growing army of landless, or almost landless, labourers…dependent on wages alone for their livelihood'.[13] Buchanan Sharp has claimed that by the time of the revolution the artisans in the major manufacturing areas of rural England—clothmaking, mining and iron making—'depended largely on wages provided by capitalist employers': 'the skilled as well as unskilled workforce was overwhelmingly propertyless and dependent on wages'.[14]

There is a problem about the proportion of wage earners in the population as a whole. R H Tawney calculated that 'except in those parts of the country…where a large population was employed in textile industries, the family entirely dependent for its livelihood upon wage labour was in rural districts the exception…though the proportion of the people employed as wage labourers was growing, the "typical" workman was not a wage labourer, but a small master craftsman or a landholding peasant'.[15] Conservative estimates put the proportion of wage workers at between a quarter and a third of both rural and urban populations. Everitt judges that, in Tudor and early Stuart periods, 'England still remained an overwhelmingly peasant community: a land of small family farms where outside labour was only occasionally employed at peak periods.' Donald

Woodward concludes that 'English society during the 16th and early 17th centuries had not yet become a predominantly wage earning society...', and A L Beier observes that '...the line between working for wages and being self employed was a fine one: the person who worked purely for cash wages was probably exceptional'.[16]

The last observation introduces the key problem: the number of persons in receipt of wages may have been higher or lower than the proportions suggested, but the question is, how many were wholly dependent on wages? Many relied on wages for only part of their working lives, as servants and journeymen, or for only part of the year, like the small peasants who provided seasonal labour for the larger farmers. Most wage earners were not entirely dependent on wages for their livelihood: they had a little land and/or rights to pasture a few animals on the common lands, where they could also take wood or dig peat for fuel (ie common rights). There was a narrow, perhaps indistinguishable, line between the small farmer who supplemented the resources of his land with wage labour for larger farmers, and the farm labourer who supplemented his wages with the resources of a small plot of land and/or common rights. Many small farmers, notably in pastoral and forested regions, added to their resources by working part of their time in various manufactures, and many artisans in manufactures eked out their wages with the resources from the possession of some land and/or common rights.[17] Gramsci and Shanin located most of these categories of wage earners socially and ideologically with the peasantry: the former described agricultural labourers as 'for the most part simply peasants without land...and not the workers of an agricultural industry developed through concentration of capital and the division of labour'; and the latter accounted as marginally a 'peasant', 'an agricultural labourer lacking a fully fledged farm' and a rural craftsman who had 'little or no land' but whose work was provided by agriculture.[18] But Lenin related all these categories of wage earners to a developing proletariat, describing them as 'semi-proletarians, or dwarf peasants, ie those who obtain their livelihood partly as wage labourers. In agricultural and industrial capitalist enterprises and partly by working their own, or rented, plots of land, which provide only a part of the means of subsistence for their families'; adding that 'the lot of these semi-proletarians is a very hard one'.[19]

The retention by small peasants, artisans and labourers of

85

some land and common rights underpinned the survival and continuation of the traditional economy and society. The supplement of wage labour in agriculture or manufacture enabled independent smallholding peasants to survive, and agrarian resources allowed artisans to retain a degree of independence because they were not wholly reliant on wages.

The 'putting out system' in manufacture, by which a merchant put out work to a small producer, such as weaving, or a larger producer put out work to a smaller one, such as spinning, was a means for extending the penetration of capitalism and making small producers dependent on capitalists. But it is difficult to discern the point at which the small producer was transformed into a proletarian.

The small producer in manufacture who became dependent on a merchant, who provided him with his raw materials and paid him for his finished product, is often regarded as equivalent to a wage worker, de facto a wage worker.[20] Albert Soboul, in his study of sans-culottes in the French Revolution, differentiated between the 'independent craftsman' and the 'dependent craftsman'. The latter headed his own concern, possessed his own tools and machines, and hired labour. He appeared to be an employer but was really a wage earner, strictly dependent on the merchant who supplied him with the raw materials and distributed the finished article.[21] However, the 'dependent craftsman' still possessed his own workshop and instruments of production, he was the patriarchal master of his workforce, he controlled his own time and methods of work, and he owned the product of his labour. Soboul made the point that he did not regard himself as a wage worker but identified himself with the independent small producers.[22] But when the artisan was tied to a single merchant-manufacturer, who put out work to him, and when he contracted to supply articles for fixed sums of money, he may be regarded as employed at a piece rate wage. It is argued that he had then ceased to own the product of his labour but sold his labour power itself.[23] That development, which was essential to the advance of capitalism, was becoming familiar at the time of the English Revolution, for Thomas Hobbes observed that labour was 'a commodity exchanged for benefit' and that 'poor people sell their labour'.[24] But in the cases under consideration, capital remained external to the process of production, which was taken over from the pre-capitalist mode, and the capitalist did not take direct control of that process.[25] Proletarianisation 'moves workers from a position of control over the organisation of their work to one in which that organisation is imposed from outside. At its most fundamental, the rise of a modern working class is the saga of power in the workshops, and proletarianisation is the process that deprives workers of their power'.[26] Under the 'putting-out system' the small producer lost a great deal of his independence but he was not fully proletarianised.

The crucial issue for Marx was possession of the means of production, which did not cover just tools or machines but also the organisation of production and working conditions.[27] Under the 'putting-out system' the small producer 'remained connected with the means of production he used,' as Marx put it, 'just as a snail is connected with its shell.' The full development of capitalism required the means of production to be separated from the producer and converted into capital, and for the capitalist to become the owner of the means of production and thus appropriate the labour power of the producer. Proletarianisation was a dual process in which the producer came to own only his labour power, which became a commodity that he sold on the market to the capitalist, and the means of production were taken from the producer and became capital confronting him.[28]

Marx's explanation of the transition from feudalism to capitalism centred on dispossessing small producers of the means of production, peasants as well as artisans, and will bear quotation at length because it contains a thesis about property which will need to be explored in the next section:

> What does the primary accumulation of capital, its historical origin amount to?... It signifies nothing other than the expropriation of the immediate producers, that is to say the making an end of private property based upon the labour of its owner... The worker's private ownership of the means of production is the basis of petty industry... Of course, this method of production is also found within the slaveholding system, within the system of serfdom, and within other dependent relationships. But it only flourishes, only manifests its full energy, only assumes its adequate and classical form, where the worker is the free private owner of the means of labour which he uses; only when the peasant owns the land he tills, and when the handicraftsman owns the tools which he handles as a virtuoso... The expropriation of the great masses of the people from the land, from the means of subsistence, and from the instruments of

labour—this terrible and grievous expropriation of the populace—comprises the prelude to the history of capital… Self earned private property, the private property that may be looked upon as grounded on a coalescence of the…independent worker, with his working conditions, is supplanted by capitalist private property, which is maintained by the exploitation of others' labour, but of labour which, in a formal sense, is free.[29]

Resistance to proletarianisation

Marx saw the transition as extending from the 15th to the end of the 18th century in England. The resistance of small producers to this process, which may be rightly termed a class struggle, was sustained throughout this period and formed a key element in the English Revolution of the 17th century. It needs to be added to Marx's account that from the 15th to the 18th century small peasants, artisans and labourers 'often fought a very successful class struggle' against feudal landlords and village bourgeoisie to secure for a time the survival of many smallholdings and common rights. Landless or near landless peasants struggled to retain their common rights in order to avoid becoming completely dependent on wages and losing their independent way of life.[30]

The agitations amongst the rank and file of the London guilds and companies in the 1640s and 1650s were a major element in the revolution. Sometimes they referred to their support for parliament in the civil war and sometimes they invoked radical political principles. These were not, as Margaret James thought, struggles between 'a growing class of wage earners' and their employers, but struggles in the defence of the independence of small producers. Some producers enlarged their operations by increasing their labour force, taking on more apprentices than permitted under the rules of the companies and employing unapprenticed labour, and so developing towards becoming capitalist manufacturers. Tailors protested in 1649 that 'divers rich men of our trade by taking over great multitudes of apprentices do weaken the poorer sort of us', and printers complained that 'some few of the rich' masters 'oppress the lesser printers…by keeping large numbers of apprentices'. The focal point of the struggles in the London companies was the demand of small masters for the enforcement of the regulations which required a seven year apprenticeship and set limits to the number of apprentices a master might employ. The intention was to prevent larger masters from taking work away from the smaller masters, who would be liable to lose their independent businesses and have to work for the larger producers, and from hindering journeymen setting up their own businesses, so forcing them to work as wage earners all their lives. Small masters might be driven out of their craft altogether and have to seek unskilled labouring jobs. London weavers said that 'at the beginning of the war many of us and our servants engaged for the parliament', but when 'we returned to follow our callings, we can get no employment', so that many hundreds were driven to become 'porters, labourers, water bearers, chimney sweepers, salt criers and coalmen'.[31] The decline of guild control was a precondition for the development of industrial capitalism, and the fact that the enforcement of guild or company regulations was an issue in the 1640s and 1650s points to the transition to capitalism being an 'issue' in the revolution.

The dispossession of peasants and artisans from the means of production was a precondition for capitalist development, but, paradoxically, the survival of an agrarian base for many farm labourers and manufacturing workers also facilitated capitalist development. Smallholders provided a reservoir of labour for capitalist farmers and capitalist manufacturers, furnishing them with a supply of labour which could be readily contracted or expanded in response to movements of the market, and at a lower cost because not wholly dependent on wages for their subsistence. The increasing numbers dependent for part or all of their livelihood on money wages, low as they were, injected modest additions of purchasing power into the economy and so contributed to the self sustaining growth of the home market, which was another precondition for capitalist development.[32]

A distinction must be made between the class of independent small producers (generally termed at the time 'the middle sort of people') and the class of full time wage labourers (generally included under the designation 'the poor'). The former comprised peasants who owned or rented a farm which was sufficient for their subsistence without having to resort to working for wages to any major extent or at all, and artisans who possessed their own workshops, raw materials and tools. It was from amongst the class of independent small producers that the main driving force of the revolution probably came, and amongst whom the radicals certainly found their chief strength. But revolutions commonly begin with alliances between diverse social groups against an existing regime, and as the revolution develops the different and conflicting interests of those groups emerge. In the English Revolution opposition to Charles I and the royalists brought together a few aristocrats, some gentry and merchants, numerous farmers and artisans as well as labourers, leading historians to jump to the conclusion that it was not a class struggle. But it was with the progress of the revolution that class differences and class conflicts emerged, shaping the course and outcome of the revolution.[33]

In the present context the proposition is that initially in the English Revolution there was cooperation between radical elements of the 'middle sort' and rebellious elements of the labouring poor. Early on it was observed in the anti-royalist riots of 1642 that 'this fury was not only in the rabble, but many of the better sort behaved themselves as if there had been a dissolution of all government'.[34] The gulf between small producers and their workers was not great, at least economically. Richard Baxter wrote of cloth manufacture at Kidderminster in Worcestershire, where he was minister: 'Three or four of the richest thriving masters of the trade got but about £500 or £600 in 20 years, and it may be lose £100 of it at once by an ill debtor. The generality of the master workmen lived but a little better than their journeymen (from hand to mouth), but only that they laboured not altogether so hard'.[35] The 'middle sort', where they were strong enough, gave leadership to the poor. John Corbet, a minister in Gloucestershire, recorded the support of the 'middle sort' there for parliament in the civil war, notably in the cloth manufacturing districts, and said that 'the poor and needy...observed those men by whom those manufactures were maintained that kept them alive'.[36] The common action of the 'middle' and 'poorer' sorts may have been rooted in shared antagonism towards the ruling class, as expressed by Laurence Clarkson, a tailor, in 1647:

> For who are the oppressors, but the nobility and gentry; and who are oppressed, is not the yeoman, the farmer, the tradesman, and the labourer? Then consider, have you not chosen oppressors to redeem you from oppression?... It is naturally inbred in the major part of the nobility and gentry...to judge the poor but fools, and themselves wise, and therefore when you the commonalty call a parliament,

they are confident such must be chosen that are noblest and richest…but…reason affirms…these are not your equals, neither are
these sensible of the burden that lies upon you; for indeed…your
slavery is their liberty, your poverty is their prosperity.[37]

The question, however, will have to be explored subsequently,
how far such alliance was sustainable in face of divergent class
interests between small producers and wage workers.

Small producers as peasants were driven by anxiety to retain
their land, and as artisans by concern to avoid becoming dependent on wealthy merchants, and both groups by fear of being
reduced to wage workers. The radicals developed an ideology
that the producer had property in his own labour and its fruits.
This expressed the class consciousness of small producers in their
struggle with the ruling class and its institutions, for it proclaimed
that the rent of the landlord, the tithes paid to the church, and
the taxes levied by the state were appropriated from the labours
of the producers, and this was sanctioned and enforced by the
coercion of the law. The wealth of the rich, they said, was created
by the labours of the poor. The Buckinghamshire Levellers
declared, 'When a man has got bread, viz necessaries by his
labour, it is his bread,' and he should not have to pay 'tribute
out of his labour' in rents and dues to a landlord who does not
work for it. The rulers 'do likewise extort away the labours of
their poor brethren, and take out the bread out of their mouths,
and from their poor wives and children, by their unreasonable,
unlawful, unjust and wicked' taxes and tithes, 'as that the flour
of those industrious men's labours are boulted out from them, and
only the bran left them to feed on'.[38] A manifesto of 1647 against
tithes declared, 'We have a natural right unto our goods gotten by
the daily labour of our hands, and so we have a right unto our
crop of corn, as it is the fruit of our proper stock of money and
year's labour'.[39]

Marx saw this doctrine, that the small producer had property
in his own labour, as arising from the petty mode of production, whose defining characteristic was that the small producer
owned the means of production as his private property.[40]
C B Macpherson, however, argued, in his discussion of the
Levellers, that this doctrine arose from the development of capitalism and provided a conception of property appropriate to the
establishment of 'a full capitalist market society', because the

notion that the producer owned his labour implied that he could sell his labour, and so suited the capitalist mode of production which regarded labour as a commodity.[41] Macpherson is right that 'the free alienation of property, including the property in one's labour, by sale and purchase is an essential element of capitalist production', but he strains the evidence regarding the Levellers. A distinction needs to be made between selling labour and selling the fruits of labour, but Macpherson confuses the two. The Levellers were not talking about wage labourers, who did sell their labour, but about small producers who were resisting the fruits of their labour being taken from them. This is why the Levellers defended private property, which was the foundation of the independence of the small producers, protecting their ownership of the means of production.[42]

The livelihood of the craftsman or artisan depended on the difference between his costs of production and the price at which he could sell his wares. Many craftsmen and artisans, rather than selling directly to the consumer, were selling increasingly to merchants for retail or export.

> It is very strange to my understanding, that one man should do the work, and another man receive the wages; I mean, that the honest clothier who has toiled much in the making of his cloth, shall not have the benefit to sell it here for his own gain...but...must make sale to them, in whose power it is to give him what price they please, whereby he is cheated of the fruits of his labour.[43]

London artisans during the revolution addressed class conscious manifestos to the rich merchants of the city:

> When with extreme care, rackt credit and hard labour ourselves and servants have produced our manufactures, with what cruelty have you wrought, and still work upon our necessities, and enrich yourselves upon our extremities, offering yea frequently buying our work for less than (you know) the stuff whereof it was made cost us; by which the like unconscionable means in grinding the faces of the poor, and advancing yourselves on our ruins, most of you rich citizens come to your wealth.[44]

> You of the city that buy our work must have your tables furnished, and your cups overflow; and therefore will give us little or nothing for our work, even what you please, because you know we must sell for monies to set our families on work, or else we

famish. Thus our flesh is that whereupon you rich men live, and wherewith you deck and adorn yourselves.[45]

Again these radicals were not speaking for wage labourers but for small producers, who sold the fruits of their labour, not their labour power itself. They were not employees but employers—the references in the manifestos to 'servants' and 'families' (the latter term denoted 'households' and so included living-in servants and apprentices) indicate that they employed apprentices and journeymen. The merchant was taking a middleman's profit, as the intermediary between producer and consumer, and incurring the odium that middlemen traditionally attracted. The independence of the producer was being reduced by cutting him off from the market both for his raw materials and for the distribution of his finished goods, and the conflict was between small manufacturing producers and merchants.[46] A manifesto of the printers asserted the value of small producers above that of merchants:

For without the clothier what were the draper, without the hatmaker where were the haberdashers, and without the printer where were the bookseller? Yea, having the clothier what need (necessarily) is there of the draper…and having the printer there is no fear of wanting books though there were no bookseller.[47]

Divergence between small producers and wage workers

The degree of independence of the small producers varied: a few peasants and craftsmen were advancing to become capitalists, notably by extending production for the market by means of the employment of more wage labour, and others were sinking into wage workers. Petty production contained within itself 'the embryo of capitalist relations'.[48] This raises the Marxist question whether the small producers constituted a class or, if they did, how far they could develop clear class consciousness and effective class action.[49] There was an ambiguity in their position. As owners of the means of production they were exploiters of labour and thus had something in common with larger scale exploiters of labour like landlords and merchants, but as manual workers directly engaged in production and exploited by landlords and merchants, they had sympathy with the wage dependent poor who suffered oppression. I think that

93

they were a class. Classes are always changing and the class of small producers was becoming split between those hopeful of rising to become larger owners and bigger employers and those fearful of being forced down into wage workers. 'The germs both of proletarian and industrial capitalist class consciousness were already contained in the craftsmen', wrote Kautsky.[50] It is a decisive factor in the English Revolution that the 'middle sort' were divided between elements that favoured developments which we see now as facilitating the growth of capitalism and elements hostile towards those developments, and the revolution was a crucial phase in crystallising a proto-bourgeoisie and a proto-proletariat.

The dividing line between small producer and proletarian was the possession or not of the means of production, and for many poor peasants and artisans this involved whether or not they had some land and/or common rights. Struggles against enclosures, which divided common land and wastes into individual holdings, continued throughout the revolution. But the leaders of the revolution came down in favour of enclosures.[51] This reflected the changed attitude of the better off peasant farmers, who were evolving into capitalist farmers. Roger B Manning sees the conflict over enclosures as being 'between lord and tenants on the one hand, and cottagers and landless persons on the other'. Buchanan Sharp maintains:

> The better sort began to distance themselves from the poor in a variety of ways including acceptance of enclosure as a positive social good that would eliminate, if not poverty, at least the attractiveness of their parishes to the poor. Limiting access to commons would enable control to be exercised over the poor. Elimination of the waste would prevent an increase in the number of idle and disorderly poor.

(The wastes attracted squatters who scratched a living from its resources as an alternative to regular wage labour or beggary.) At enclosure the lords of manors and their tenants—yeomen and husbandmen—were amply recompensed with allotments of enclosed land in place of their rights of common. But smallholders, landless cottagers and rural artisans were inadequately compensated for their loss of access to the commons and wastes, or not at all, and lost their cushion against dependence on wage labour. John Walter writes of a reordering of the relationships of the 'middling sort' with other social groups. The larger farmers ceased to resist enclosure, 'as long as it accommodated their interests', because 'agrarian capitalism' was becoming the foundation of 'their growing wealth and power'. Seen from the other side, by J M Neeson, enclosure tore away the mask of shared interests and revealed the different interests of poorer and richer villagers; it brought about a growing separation of classes and taught the smallholders and landless labourers, who 'lost their winter fuel, the grazing for a cow or a few sheep, the feed for pigs and geese', 'the new reality of class relations' of an emerging village bourgeoisie and proletariat: 'Enclosure had a terrible but instructive visibility.' Nevertheless, ambiguity persisted, for bigger farmers, who paid the largest proportion of the poor rates, might still oppose enclosure because they feared that the loss of common rights would reduce their poorer neighbours to dependence on poor relief.[52] During the revolution, partly as a response to popular revolts and partly out of fear of strengthening the radical movements such as the Levellers, Diggers and Fifth Monarchists, efforts were made to reduce the adverse impact of enclosures on the poor and to remedy some of their complaints.[53]

The Levellers said little about wage labourers. One of the few references in their manifestos was a call that 'care be taken forthwith to advance the native commodities of this nation, that the poor may have better wages for their labour, and that manufactures may be increased'.[54] These phrases are significant, for they expressed the demand of the radicals in general for the poor to be set to work, which reflected a shift promoted by the revolutionaries from regarding the poor as a burden on the community— on the 'middle sort' who had to pay poor rates for their relief— to regarding them as a potential asset which could be employed to increase the production of manufactures.[55] And so, as one pamphlet said, enrich the nation 'by encouraging all their labours and industry, advancing home-made commodities' whose export could thus be increased many times over in a few years.[56] This policy sprang in part from humanitarian concern for the poor but it was conducive to the development of capitalist enterprise.

The law relating to debt was a more pressing problem than wages for the Levellers and most radicals, and the difficulties of recovering money from those who could afford to pay, and the sufferings in prisons of those who could not afford to pay, were close to the hearts of small producers, for they were constantly involved both in giving credit and in borrowing money to stock their farms or workshops.[57] It must be borne in mind that many of the 'middle sort' were employers of labour and had an interest in keeping wages down. Real wages may have increased during the 1650s,[58] and amidst all the complaints about wages being too low, there were those in this period who protested that they were too high: the wages of servants 'being advanced to such an extraordinary height, that they are likely ere long to be masters and their masters servants, many poor husbandmen being forced to pay as much to their servants for wages as to their landlords for rent'.[59]

Resistance by wage labourers

Although one pamphleteer said that 'the only cry of honest poor men is that they want employment',[60] it does appear that 'low wages were more important than unemployment in causing hardship', but the latter often resulted from under-employment (the low number of days of work in the year).[61] Some radicals did speak up for the wage labourers. John Cooke, a barrister who was counsel for the prosecution at the trial of the king, expressed concern that the wages of 'the poor labouring man that has nothing but what he gets by his day labour' were insufficient to feed his family, so that 'he must beg, steal, or starve.' Admittedly he was writing at a time of rising food prices, but he noted the variability of wage earnings, sometimes three shillings a week, sometimes two shillings, 'and some weeks not 12 pence'.[62] The famous radical pamphlet *Tyranipocrit* stressed the extreme economic inequalities and the indifference of the well to do for the plight of the poor:

As for some to have so many hundred pounds a year for doing of nothing, or for executing of some needless office, or to oversee and command others, etc and a poor labouring man must work for three or four pence a day, and we uncharitable partial wretches can behold all this and be silent, and we pass it over as a matter not worthy of consideration.

'And we will pay them poorly' to till our land, 'and when they have done it, we will esteem them almost so much as we do of our hounds and horses, and yet we will be faithful Christians, and we will rule all Christendom'.[63] Another tract said that:

Those men that have nothing but their labour to subsist on either by ploughing, threshing, hedging, and such like country employments, are little better than slaves. Let them be never so laborious, their wages is so little, that they are never in all their lives able to lay up anything for the subsistence of their families after their death; and therefore it generally comes to pass, that if country labourers die while their children are young and unable to work for themselves, they must unavoidably be relieved by the alms of the parish, which as the laws are executed is sad livelihood.[64]

A Digger protested that such men must 'go with cap in hand, and bended knee, to gentlemen and farmers, begging and entreating to work with them for eight pence or ten pence a day, which does give them an occasion to tyrannise over poor people'.[65] The belief that the producer owned his own labour passed from the 'middle sort' to the wage labourers:

Though we keep ourselves close to our hard labours, breaking our due and necessary rest which should refresh us, whereby our lives become a burden to us, and yet our careful and diligent labour will afford us no other than a distracted, languishing and miserable life. For how can it be otherwise, seeing we cannot enjoy the benefit of our labours ourselves, but for the maintenance of idle persons, slow bellies who reign and ride over the common people in every parish as Gods and Kings.[66]

Gerrard Winstanley, the Digger leader, perceptively discerned that the poor had their labour power taken from them. He visualised the landless poor as a conquered people who had been dispossessed by their conquerors (the ruling class), who forced them to labour for wages and as 'slaves to work for them that had taken their property of their labours from them by the sword' and 'at this very day poor people are forced to work in some places for four, five and six pence a day; in other places for eight, ten and 12 pence a day, for such small prizes...that their earnings cannot find them bread for their family.' If they were reduced to homeless vagrants they were whipped, and if they stole to support themselves they were hanged.[67]

At the height of the revolution the Diggers campaigned for the abolition of wage labour. Their alternative was for the poor to regain possession of the main means of production in their society—the land. Their aim was to abolish rents and wages and to form communes in which the poor would cultivate the land collectively and share its produce according to their needs. This attracted some land-holding peasants who began to form such communities on common and waste lands (a radical alternative to enclosure into individual holdings for private gain), but the movement was crushed by force by landlords and richer farmers before it had time to grow to any size, though it may have had many hidden sympathisers among the poor.[68]

The increase of the number of full time wage workers and their degradation probably fostered among them an approach to consciousness of being a distinct class, and created a potential for class conflict in those areas where capitalism was taking control. Alan Everitt says that on large farms where wage labourers were employed in production for the market, the farmers' eyes became 'fixed firmly on prices and profits', and they 'ceased to think of their labourers as their own "folk" and neighbours' but 'as mere employees, to be taken on or dismissed at pleasure, as commercial prudence alone dictated'. In such a situation 'the frictions between masters and men were often acute' and from the time of the civil war took on more of a relationship between 'antagonistic classes'.[69] In clothmaking areas where some of the most militant support for parliament appeared in the civil war, J A Sharpe discerns amongst the wage workers 'a nascent class consciousness' and outbreaks of hostility towards 'their social superiors in general'.[70] And Buchanan Sharp judges that in such areas there appeared 'sentiments approaching class hatred' and 'violent outbreaks of what can only be called class hatred for the wealthy'.[71]

At the same time the most visible signs of impoverishment were crowds of beggars in the streets and gangs of vagrants on the roads. The landless poor migrated to the wastes and forests where they squatted illegally, or to London where they hoped to find casual employment but were often obliged to become beggars, thieves or prostitutes. In London, as in other large cities of pre-industrial Europe, unskilled casual labour accumulated, as dockers, porters, road sweepers, water carriers, and navvies.[72] During the English Revolution they may have provided recruits for London 'mobs', but Christopher Hill regards them as 'basically non-political', and they may correspond to what Marx described as the 'lumpenproletariat'.[73] Some of them died in the streets from hunger or exposure.[74]

Hill stresses the hostility towards wage labour in 17th century

England, and the strategies evolved to evade or escape it. This may be regarded as an early manifestation of a proletarian ideology, which was incompatible with capitalism, but as capitalism developed, wage earners initiated trade unions and industrial action, which meant a de facto acceptance of wage work, recognition that capitalism was an established system and efforts to improve their lot under it.[75]

The revolution emerged from a civil war and the victorious parliamentarian army, the revolutionary New Model Army, carried through the execution of the king, the abolition of the monarchy and the House of Lords, and the establishment of a republic, which it defended at home and abroad for ten years. The success and survival of the revolution depended on the army, which became 'the salvation, but also the ruler of the republic'.[76] Deployed successfully to crush challenges from the left and the right, the army became incapable either of moving forward to more radical social reforms or of converting itself into a more conservative regime with broad civilian support from aristocrats and bourgeois. And there were frictions within the army's own internal structures.

Marx observed in *Grundrisse* that 'the first form of wage labour was soldiers' pay'.[77] The rank and file of the New Model Army formed the largest concentration of wage labourers in the country. Private soldiers in the infantry were paid eight pence a day—a common wage for agricultural labourers—but the officers, most of whom came from higher social groups, were very well paid and had opportunities to acquire land and lucrative positions in civil administration. The rank and file were only temporarily wage earners: many were recruited from small producers and after military service returned to farms or craft workshops; but others were 'tinkers, pedlars and vagrants that have no dwelling, and such of whom no account can be given'—the sort of people that Hill describes as resisters to wage labour.[78] The army was separate from the system of production and cannot be equated with capitalist relations, for the soldiers were mostly conscripts and not labourers freely selling their labour power, and they were not paid by capitalists but by the state.[79] Nevertheless, the soldiers were wage labourers and the officers were effectively their employers. Everitt suggests that the bringing together of different social classes into close proximity in the army focused the differences between rich and poor that existed in society at

99

large.[80] The tensions in society between wage labourers and their masters were reproduced in the army, where the proneness of that relationship to generate class consciousness and class conflict was demonstrated. This may have been a major influence on the outcome of the revolution. This is not say that relations between officers and men were uniformly and continuously bad, far from it: the New Model Army would not have been so effective a fighting machine if that had been so, and officers who looked after their men, who were good at their job and 'affable' (the quality plebeians valued in their superiors) were liked or respected. But there was another side: the life was hard and they were at the mercy of their officers, whose authority was supported by strict discipline and cruel punishments.

There were manifestos during the English Revolution which purported to speak for the private soldiers and which presented a picture of conflict between officers and men. They stressed the hardships of the service: 'night by night upon the guard'; long marches and hard lodgings where they slept on bare boards or on the ground in the open; poorly shod, clothed and fed, and their wage a 'small pittance' which was no more than would keep them from starving, that is when they could get it, for it was often in arrears. They described it as a 'dog's life' and themselves as 'poor and beggarly'. Then they spoke of tyrannical officers:

> Must we not go and run when they will have us, and whither they will send us? Must we not lie at their doors day and night like dogs to watch and guard them... Are we not scorned and abused, and kicked like dogs by them, as if we were the very scum of the world in their esteem?... I appeal to my fellow soldiers, I mean especially the foot...whether we are not used more like beasts than men, like slaves than Christians.

They contrasted their poverty with their officers' wealth. They pointed out that the officers gained their honours as a result of the sweat and courage of the private soldiers, the rewards for whose labours went mainly to the officers. 'An officer undergoes little or no hardship at all' but the common soldier:

> undergoes great hardship with hard labour night and day... It is not unknown to you what perils and danger we have [undergone] under you during the whole war, how we that are the private soldiers are they who fought and conquered the kingdom, and yet our officers

they have reaped the honour and profit of all our enterprises and sufferings... They have been recompensed and rewarded and we continue still in our old condition of want and misery, and if we have gotten but a red coat, which is a fool's livery, we have thought ourselves sufficiently rewarded and recompensed...

The strength, the honour and being of the officer...does consist in the arm of the soldier. Is it not the soldier that endures the heat and burden of the day, and performs that work whereof the officers bear the glory and name? For what is, or what can the officers do without the soldier? [81]

The officers exploited the labour of the soldiers to gain wealth and power for themselves. The language of the protests echoed the experience of wage labourers in the wider society. Thus there was expressed in microcosm in the New Model Army a class conflict in society at large during the English Revolution.

The soldiers were given their arrears of pay in the form of debentures, but in desperate need of ready cash they sold them to their officers at large discounts. A pamphlet addressed by an army man to 'his loving fellow soldiers' in January 1660 protested:

Did not most of those officers...purchase your debentures (the price of blood) from two shillings to a noble [six shillings and eight pence] in the pound to enrich themselves and perpetuate your slavery? And through their cruelty many of our fellow soldiers, who were wounded in battle and made unserviceable, with wives and children starved in the streets for want of bread, while they lorded over you tyrant like. Now examine yourselves whether when you have demanded your pay, you were not had before court martials and hanged to all your shames, while they robbed you and the commonwealth of your dues.[82]

For instance, on 18 February 1660 two soldiers were publicly hanged at Charing Cross and four others given from 21 to 40 lashes on their bare backs for a mutiny over pay.[83]

In a political army many of the rank and file demonstrated political consciousness in the 1640s: in the 1650s that political consciousness bred disillusion with the revolution. In 1659 *The Sentinels Remonstrance* declared, 'The soldiery have since the beginning of these late unnatural wars...hazarded their blood...for promoting equity and justice.' After they 'did with loyal hearts and hands endure' and undergo cheerfully all 'hazardous and hard encounters' they became masters of the field 'Then was it our expectation to see liberty flourish.' But they had raised 'self seeking men' to power, who have cheated them and the people, and subjected all the nation to new oppressions and tyrannies. 'Thus have we lived to abolish the tyrannies and oppression of past times, but never expected to have erected and established worse as their successors'.[84] Thus in the crisis of 1659-60 class antagonism between privates and officers, and disillusionment with the results of the revolution amongst some of the rank and file, and apolitical attitudes of others, meant that when some officers attempted to defend the republic and to resist moves towards the restoration of the monarchy, not many soldiers rallied to them.

Most of them probably believed that officers were only interested in power and wealth for themselves. The cause of liberty, they may have felt, had been betrayed again and again by their officers, and the revolution had done nothing for the private soldier or to improve the lot of the poor in general. As a consequence the door was opened to the return of the monarchy, the House of Lords, and the Church of England, unopposed by the army.

Peasants who resisted enclosures and loss of common rights —some of whom supported parliament in the civil war in expectation that it would help them—found in the 1650s that the new regime endorsed enclosures and the erosion of common rights. In 1656 a radical MP, Luke Robinson, speaking up for the commoners of the Forest of Dean, warned:

> We promised Englishmen freedom, equal freedom... Did we not make the people believe that we fought for their liberty. Let us not deceive them of their expectation. Is it not by their hands and successes that our interest remains; that we sit here? Let us not forget it, lest we be laid aside ourselves, upon the same account that former powers were laid aside.[85]

In 1659 riots against enclosures in the Forest of Dean and Enfield Chase led to reports that at one of their meetings 'some people of Dean professed that their hard usage at the hands of parliament would force them to turn cavalier', and to allegations of the rioters at Enfield 'making great shouts and declaring for Charles Stuart'.[86] But too much reliance should not be placed on this evidence.

Marx and Engels observed that in a bourgeois revolution the opponents of the old order claim to speak and act for 'the people', but when they win power it becomes clear that they represent 'the particular interest of a particular class', and popular opposition develops against them with the aim of 'a more decisive and more radical negation of the previous conditions of society'.[87] The richer of the small producers were developing into a capitalist class and economic progress of the 1650s tended towards a coalescence of the interests of aristocrats and gentry with the interests of the emerging bourgeoisie.[88] The rest of the 'middle sort' remained anchored in the outlook of small producers and differentiated themselves from the labourers and beggars. The potential alliance of the poorer of the small producers, who feared becoming wage earners or were already partly dependent on wages, with the wage labourers, did not materialise. The emerging proletariat was not sufficiently developed to mount its own political challenge to the bourgeois compromise with the old order, or to extend the revolution, but sufficiently developed to frighten the bourgeoisie into acceptance of the return to political power of the old ruling class, on the foundation that they both 'had a common interest in keeping in subjection the great working mass of the nation' and in harmony with capitalist development.[89] In a bourgeois revolution, wrote Trotsky, 'that class which sacrifices most for the success of the revolution and hopes the most from it, receives the least of all... The disappointment of the masses follows quickly' and could lead to a second revolution, but 'more than once in history' this disappointment has 'become the starting point of a victorious counter-revolution'.[90] The latter happened in the English Revolution. The disillusionment of plebeians with the immediate results of the revolution did not provoke them to further revolutionary activity but to the abandonment of revolutionary activity. The counter-revolution, however, was only partly successful.

CHAPTER 6

Postmodernism and British history

Mark O'Brien

In the decades following the Second World War the influence of Marxism in academic history writing was pronounced. Some of the key names in the fields of working class and social history were drawn from the tradition, in particular, of the British Communist Party. Such figures as Hobsbawm, Postgate, Dobb, Hilton, Thompson, Briggs and Saville, whether remaining within the Stalinist tradition or working in negative reaction to it, were responsible for some of the most important scholarly works and popularisations of the history of capitalism and of the British working class. It was such historians also who, after the impact of the suppression of the Hungarian working class by Soviet tanks in 1956, began to look for new directions in history writing—in the setting up of the History Workshop, for example, in the pages of new journals such as *Past and Present* and in the school of historiography that took the name of 'history from below'.

Whatever we might say about the political distortions represented by the Stalinist tradition—and there certainly was some very bad history writing associated with it—the fact remains that at their best the British Marxist historians provided an important paradigm of historical research and enquiry. For those working within the tradition as well as those working outside or even in opposition to it, it provided a reference point by which historians had to take their bearings. Economic history was seen as being an essential part of a proper account of past social experience. Social movements, protest and resistance were accorded legitimacy as

105

areas of academic discussion. There was a general consensus that 'class' was an indispensable tool in social analysis.

This general consensus of a broadly 'materialist' historiography, however, is under determined and sustained attack:

> Across the 'developed' industrial world, class as an organising and legitimising political identity no longer has the assured place it once...seemed to occupy; while observers of all persuasions have been disorientated by the swift and remorseless collapse of regimes of avowedly Marxist inspiration, and the fragmentation of both liberalism and social democracy in the absence of the communist 'other'.[1]

The malaise of academic Marxism, which has been marked since the collapse of the Eastern European regimes, has been compounded by the rise of postmodernism as an aggressive and self confident intellectual fashion. The influence of postmodernism has been influential for some time in departments of art and literature. In more recent years, however, it has been mounting a challenge within the field of social history. The methodological issues thrown up by this challenge revolve particularly around the subject of working class consciousness in the 19th century. More specifically the debate turns on accounts of the shift in working class thinking from the militant Chartist years of the 1840s to the moderate liberal politics of the 1860s and the later years of the era of Victorian reform.

It is the intention of this article to precis the postmodernist argument in the context of historiography and then to test its methodology against the real history of the working class experience of the 19th century.

Postmodernist 'history'

A number of related themes are central to the postmodernist argument about the way in which we interpret history. The first is that we cannot talk of history as having any foundations which are independent of consciousness and of how people expressed themselves. Any attempt to ground a historical analysis in a broader definition of society which is independent of the contemporary opinion of the time is ruled out. Objective starting points in any account of history such as 'class structure' or 'economic relations' or even 'material conditions' are rejected as artificial impositions upon the social experience of the people who lived at the time. Patrick Joyce, very much a leading protagonist of the postmodernist group, puts it like this:

> The categories of the material and the social are…idealised or essentialised 'foundations', unable to bear the weight resting upon them. The narratives that write the history of these foundational categories—the liberal ones as much as the Marxist—stand revealed for the modernist 'grand narrative' project they are.[2]

> From a postmodern viewpoint, 'class', alongside categories like 'society' and 'economy', but also 'reason', the 'self', and so on, are all seen as exemplifications of a modernity that, as we have seen, takes them to be the 'foundations' of knowledge.[3]

For these historians there is no validity in any reference to factors which are independent of language and consciousness. Economic and material factors are rejected. Joyce even goes on to argue, following an American academic, William Sewell, that the stress on the 'material' in Marxism is symptomatic of hangover from 19th century Christian thought:

> The split between the spiritual and the material emerged out of traditional Christian and aristocratic discourse…
>
> Marxists proudly proclaim their radicalism by employing an arbitrary identification of the economic as material, never realising that they have inherited the idea intact and uncriticised from traditional Christian and aristocratic discourses.[4]

It is this rejection of the 'material' that lies behind the rejection of other categories such as the 'social', 'class' and even of 'reason'. Ultimately it leads the postmodernists to question the knowability of the world and of history itself. As James Vernon puts it:

> I am not arguing that society or the real do not exist, just that we can have no knowledge of them outside discourse.[5]

For the postmodernists the 'foundationalism' of traditional history writing does not grasp the complexities of the historical process or of the ways in which people define themselves in relation to their times. Hence the need to reject also any framework which attempts to unify history or to locate historical experience within clarifying categories. Rather identities must be 'de-centred' in order to see people as they really were:

The search now is for how meanings have been produced by relations of power, rather than for 'external' or 'objective' class 'structures'. It also follows that if identity is composed through the relations of systems of difference, then it is marked by conflict, and is plural, diverse and volatile. The view of identity is one in which many 'identities' press in and react with one another (we are men and women, parents and children, members of classes and nations, modernists and postmodernists, and so on). It is a view rather at odds with many accounts of class, which tend to deal in fairly uniform and coherent identities.[6]

And finally the notion of a 'coherent' view of history is jettisoned:

A recognition of the irreducibly discursive character of the social undermines the idea of social totality. There is no overarching coherence evident in either the polity, the economy or the social system...there is no underlying structure to which they can be referred as expressions or effects. Thus with the notion of social totality goes the notion of social determination, so central to 'social history'. The certainty of a materialist link to the social is likewise broken... Responding to the anti-reductionist logic of postmodernism means, therefore, thinking about new versions of the social, ones that require historians to be the inquisitors and perhaps the executioners of the old valuations.[7]

For the postmodernists it is language which provides the key to understanding history—this is what they call the 'linguistic turn'. They make two related claims for language which go way beyond a mere sensitivity to subjective expression. The first is that what people said about themselves and the times in which they lived is the only way in which we can look at the past. In this view the utterances of people in the past must be taken literally. What people said at the time was simply the truth and we are unqualified to comment outside that framework. The second argument about language goes to the philosophical heart of the debate. It says that language was not simply the expression of the social experience of the working class—it actually defined that experience. Here, then, language is not just a way of talking about the world, it actually constructed the world in which people lived. The social experiences of particular historical periods are the result of so many 'discourses' (ways of talking about the world). It is in this sense that the postmodernists deny a social reality which is independent of how it was 'represented' at the time.

This exclusive stress on public language, on which the post-modernists insist, is being used to drive through a wholesale revision of interpretations of 19th century working class history. By concentrating on the influence of notions such as 'self reliance', the rights of the 'freeborn Englishman' and the por-trayal of the rich as an 'evil' or 'idle' class, they are able to trace unbroken historical threads which pass lightly over hugely dif-ferent historical periods. A work which is of pivotal significance for the postmodernists here is Gareth Stedman Jones's 1981 essay 'Rethinking Chartism'. Stedman Jones chooses the theme of opposition to 'Old Corruption' which was the cry of the English Radical movement from the middle of the 18th century. Old Corruption was the term used to mark out the old aristocracy who were perceived to be a sort of cancerous excrescence which dom-inated parliament and which was impeding the progress of English society towards openness and fairness for all. At the heart of the radical tradition was the idea that it was government which was the root of all evil in society. If representation could be achieved for all inequality would be eradicated:

> In England radicalism first surfaced as a coherent programme in the 1770s, and first became a vehicle for plebeian political aspi-rations from the 1790s. Its strength, indeed its definition, was a critique of the corrupting effects of the concentration of political power and its corrosive influence on a society deprived of proper means of political representation... Elements of this vocabulary went back to the revolutions of the 17th century and were reforged by those who felt excluded by the settlements of 1688 and 1714... But however much radicalism extended its scope...it could never be the ideology of a specific class. It was first and foremost a vocabulary of political exclusion whatever the character of those excluded. Thus if it became de facto the exclusive property of the 'working classes' in the 1830s and 1840s, this did not lead to a basic restructuring of the ideology itself. The self identity of rad-icalism was not that of any specific group, but of the 'people' or the 'nation' against the monopolisers of political representation and power and hence of financial or economic power.[8]

From this Stedman Jones argues that the reason for Chartism's decline was that, as political representation expanded to include   109 the working class, the language, or discourse, of radicalism became less persuasive:

> Once therefore the conviction of the totally evil character of the political system itself began to fade and distress became less pervasive, there was no independent rationale within radical ideology for antagonism towards the middle class as such... Chartism began to fail when a gulf opened up between its premisses and the perceptions of its constituency.[9]

The point is rounded off by James Vernon, another advocate of the 'linguistic turn':

> Those still excluded from the political nation, the working class, struggled to keep this Whiggish state accountable by again using civic humanist languages to redefine the constitution and redistribute political power. Although this process was temporarily halted by the state's use of conciliation and coercion, the radical libertarian critique of a corrupt, unaccountable, aristocratic state continued to resonate during the 1850s and was critical to the invention of popular Liberalism and Conservatism, as well as to the independent labour and women's politics of the 20th century.[10]

So there it is. A long tradition, developing around the central theme of a struggle for political representation stretching from the 1770s (or arguably from 1688), through the working class politics of the 1840s, to the labourism of the early 20th century embracing everything from 'popular Conservatism' to the Suffragettes and in which Gladstonian liberalism is the natural inheritor of the Chartist movement!

History in this view is about continuities. Distinctions between both periods which have quite different social and economic characters and between different social groups and classes are not only blurred, they are eradicated. Traditions too blend smoothly into one another. In *Visions of the People*,[11] for example, Joyce charts the supposed continuity from Chartism into liberalism by reference to individuals such as William Aitken and Thomas Livesy, both of Rochdale, who, after their early Chartist years, went on to be mainstream figures in the Liberal politics of the town. In similar style Joyce seeks to persuade us that strong undercurrents of liberal thought flowed also into the thinking of the socialist politics of the 1880s, the Social Democratic Federation of Hyndman and Morris getting a particular mention.

In this account 'class' and class differences have long since been pushed to the margins. 'Class' is replaced with the idea of the 'people' and the picture we are given is one of a 'populist' struggle for political representation. It is not that 'class' is completely irrelevant. It does have a role, but only as a form of identity in the 1830s and 1840s and then not again until well into the 20th century:

> The identity of 'the people' could in fact take on a class character, turning on the idea of labour as a 'working class' in conflict with capital…but it is necessary to get it in perspective as one, and probably not the greatest, among a range of possible social and political identities available to and used by the labouring populations.[12]

'Class' as a subjective construction, then, is acknowledged. 'Class' as an objective reality, reflecting an underlying social structure, is jettisoned. Economics, exploitation and the social oppression of working class life in the 19th century have been painted out. Part of the argument here also is that the rise of Chartism, and the militant working class politics in the late 1830s, had nothing to do with the Industrial Revolution. Language, ideas, symbols and 'discourse' are everything, the social and the economic, nothing.

The argument that the liberalism of the second half of the 19th century represented a continuation of the radicalism of the Chartist movement, rather than being a retreat from it, has become loud in recent years. In fact the Manchester postmodernists are part of a larger group who argue along very similar lines.[13] The conclusion which follows is that the liberalism of working class thinking and political expression did not represent the rise of a more bourgeois consciousness on the part of workers but rather was the continuation, albeit in a different form, of a populist challenge to an exclusive political establishment:

> Chartism and parliamentary radicalism were interlinked. Both movements were committed to the same political strategy, the ultimate goal of which was accountable, popular government. Such a 'strategy' eschewed 'class' politics, for the only way in which executive government could be properly monitored and controlled was through the presence of independent MPs, who pursued national rather than local objects, and who represented public rather than class or sectional interests.[14]

111

Whether they celebrate this conclusion or, like Vernon, bemoan it,[15] the underlying analysis is the same:

> Working class Liberalism was not the fruit of the 'ideological success' of 'bourgeois ideology' during the mid-Victorian decades, but rather of the institutionalisation of older and genuinely plebeian traditions.[16]

The test of history

The exclusion of the 'social' from the historical account of the working class of early industrial society, and the narrowly political focus on traditions of thought are utterly distorting. Consider the differences in the social character and social experience of the working class over this entire period. In the mid-17th century artisanal production was still a definitive feature of society in the villages and small towns of England. Artisans either worked alone or shared the space of small craft workshops. 'Industry' was limited in scale and in location by the availability of water power and tended to be found still in rural areas. The artisan owned what he had produced and then sold it. The artisan was of course exploited, perhaps ruthlessly, by the workshop owner from whom he rented space or machinery and to whom he often sold his produce. But the artisan retained some degree of control over the product of his labour and indeed the time and intensity of his labour.

The Industrial Revolution, which reached its frenzied peak in the 1830s, was as much a revolution in social relations as it was of technology. The old workshop industries were decimated and those struggling to eke out some kind of living from what remained of their markets were impoverished. The discipline in the new factories was draconian. The housing provided for workers at extortionate rents was built with no regard for health or quality of life. The overcrowded and unsanitary conditions of the time have been well documented and need no repetition here. All of these things represented a qualitatively very different kind of social experience for workers and this was reflected in the movements which developed in the period. The Chartist movement for example drew its most avid supporters from the declining craft and cottage industries, the growing primary industries of mining and iron working and from the textile mills. A movement like the Chartists could simply never have happened in the 18th century.

The reality of these economic changes and the consequent class nature of the Chartist movement also were consciously appreciated by the Chartists. Indeed after the 1832 Reform Act, seen as the 'great betrayal' perpetrated by the newly enfranchised middle classes, the reform movement split cleanly along lines of class. From that point a marked hostility towards the middle class and an insistence on working class independence prevailed within the movement. Particular hostility was aimed at the liberal and Anti Corn Law factory owners who posed as friends of the worker whilst seeking to reduce wages and maintaining a ruthless exploitation within their own mills and factories.

This awareness of class, and of a battle not just for political inclusion but also against the new capitalism, is reflected in the rhetoric and theory of the leaders:

> Leading Chartists in both the factory districts of Lancashire and Cheshire and in centres of 'artisan' production, such as Birmingham and London, articulated an unmistakable, if largely non-socialist, critique of exploitation in production. Growing out of practical experience rather than theoretical abstraction, this critique suggested that an 'unnatural' and oppressive capitalist system, based on full blown commodity production, profit maximisation, 'wage slavery', the subordination of labour to capital, and the replacement of the 'honourable' master by the 'dishonourable' capitalist 'tyrant' or 'steamlord', was becoming hegemonic within production.[17]

The terms themselves indicate the way in which political language was changing. Expressions of opposition against 'Old Corruption', drawn from the Radical tradition, were becoming infused with a new class content. Thus anger in Lancashire was aimed at the new 'millocracy' of the uncaring 'cotton lords'.

Some theorisation of exploitation is also present in the thinking and language of a number of the leaders. The 'labour theory of value' was an idea which had circulated within educated working class circles for some time. The recognition of the drive of capitalists to accumulation was also present. Of course, when we compare these ideas to the developed and integrated theories of surplus value and the necessary exploitation and profit drive essential to capitalism put forward later by Marx in *Capital*, this theorisation seems limited and trapped within a moral opposition

113

to oppression. It is unhistorical—and unfair—to do so, however. What we see here is ideas in flux, full of contradictions, but moving unmistakably towards an understanding of oppression and exploitation as being rooted in the new industrial system.

Class also is obvious in the actual activity and struggle of the Chartist movement in its different phases. We can point to the overlapping membership and activist involvement between the Chartist and trade union movements. On the run up to the 1842 general strike the speakers at working class rallies were almost always Chartists. Richard Pilling, leader of the 1842 strike and Chartist, explained with directness the need for workers to organise around the defence of wages and conditions at his trial: 'The masters conspired to kill me and I combined to keep myself alive'.[18]

In the end we can only really explain the shift from the militancy and revolutionary aspect of the working class of the late 1830s and 1840s to the conservatism and reformism of the second half of the 19th century by applying a materialist analysis to both the end of Chartism and the rise of working class liberalism. Such an analysis must employ notions such as 'class', the 'social', the economic 'base' of society as well as a stress on the active role of politics and ideology in a way which does not divorce them from the objective circumstances of the time. Such an approach cuts directly against the postmodernist account with its denial of class and its insistence on the continuity of the Radical tradition within the working class throughout the 19th century.

When we look at the high points of the Chartist movement— the events around the Convention of 1838, the Newport uprising, the 1842 strikes, 1848 —one thing which is apparent on each occasion is the vacillation of the national leadership. Their individual courage is beyond doubt and it is not the purpose here to reduce their stature in modern eyes or to minimise the enormity of their historical role. However, at each crucial moment in the course of the movement we see the leadership pushed forward up until a certain point, only to fall apart in acrimony and disarray. There is something here to be explained. Of course we can say that this was the first leadership of a mass working class movement and leave it at that. But this leads to an unfocused assessment of the Chartist leadership and, in a sense, does not do them credit. We must go deeper.

The frictions within the Chartist leadership reflected a contradiction which went to the heart of the Chartist movement itself.

Broadly speaking we can identify two distinct groupings of workers who composed the movement. There were the workers of the small cottage industries, many of whom, at the turn of the century, had been known as prosperous in their communities, but who, by the 1830s, had been forced into desperate poverty by the factory system. The second group was the new industrial proletariat of the factories and cotton mills in the growing conurbations. There were continuities between the two—the new industrial workers had themselves come from the rural areas. However, there were also important qualitative differences between them. The immiserated handloom weavers of the small scale rural industries dreamed of a return to their former prosperity. Their yearnings harked back to something of a golden age before the rise of the factory system and in this sense their faces were turned to the past. Feargus O'Connor gave brilliant expression to their feelings and they repaid him with near adoration. Other leaders, Jones and Harney for example, looked more to the proletarian part of the movement. Amongst the workers of the new cities the concerns were far more to do with wages and factory reform. The socialists of the later movement also began to see in this new class the potential for a socialist influence. Their faces were turned to the future. There was then an ideological split in the leadership. O'Connor in particular was exasperating in his obsession with the Land Scheme in the 1840s and his espousal of electoral support for the Tories. Such a leadership, put to the test, revealed this underlying fault line in squabble and indecision.

The fragmentation of the Chartist movement after 1848 must be explained on a number of levels: the experience of defeat; weariness with the everlasting petition; the failure to attract a new generation of workers in the 1840s. Most importantly though, we must understand the events of 1848. It was not the case that Chartism declined gradually as the 'perceptions of its constituency' changed. Chartism suffered defeat in 1848 and the enormity of this defeat must be grasped, along with its psychological significance both for the ruling class as well as for the working class, in order to understand the social history of the rest of the 19th century in Britain.

The year 1848 saw revolutions across Europe, against the background of economic crisis and agricultural failure. In February demonstrators for liberal reform were shot down in Paris and the response was a wave of insurrection in which political leadership came from the middle and commercial classes whilst workers dominated the streets. The impact of the revolution in France triggered revolution throughout the confederated states of Germany and Northern Italy, and throughout the Austrian and Habsburg empires. The whole of the European structure of nationality and state, imposed by the allied powers on the conclusion of the Napoleonic Wars, was shaking to its foundations.

In Britain too economic hardship was widespread, as was working class unrest. The February revolution in Paris had a sensational impact in the working class districts in Britain. Rallies were held in every part of the country to celebrate the news. The Chartist movement which had been in the doldrums for some years now found itself pushed to centre stage as its membership leapt, the circulation of its publications expanded dramatically and mass gatherings began to occur once more. Attention became focused on one particular day—10 April—the day on which the third great Chartist petition for parliamentary reform would be presented. The atmosphere intensified as reports of a 'revolutionary feeling' amongst the factory operatives in the major industrial areas came in, as well as reports of arming and drilling. The Chartist convention, meeting in the days running up to the 10th, reflected the mood as the delegates, elected from open meetings held all over the country, debated whether to meet in continuous session and in so doing pose a revolutionary challenge to the government. They debated also whether to call for demonstrations all over the country in order to spread the forces of the state as thinly as possible.

Within the convention the voices of moderation, crucially O'Brien and O'Connor, won out over those such as Jones and a number of key decisions followed which determined the outcome on the day itself. The demonstrators were to be unarmed and they were to meet at Kennington Common, south of the Thames, making it a simple matter for the authorities to block the bridges and prevent access to Westminster. Even the elevation of a single day to such particular importance in the circumstances gave advantage to a united government allowing it to steady its gaze and to aim its forces well. Jones himself was later to express regret at not having broken with O'Connor on such questions.

Amongst the ranks of the well to do general panic prevailed. The general consensus was that revolution was about to cross the Channel. In one tiny quarter, however, calm prevailed. The key

116

players within the governing circles, crucially Russell, the prime minister, and Grey, the home secretary, were sure, on the eve of the day itself, that no general disturbance would occur. They could be sure because they had grasped something that no ruling class leaders in such a situation within Britain had grasped in quite the same way before—the importance of leadership within the working class. They had learned from previous occasions such as the Peterloo Massacre, as well as from the experience of empire, the dangers of attempting to terrorise the whole of the working class or large numbers of the oppressed, and they had internalised that experience. On 9 April Grey informed Russell of a meeting that had taken place between his chief police officer and Jones and O'Connor. The two Chartist leaders had been informed of the state's preparations for the day: martial law; the mass presence of specially enrolled constables; troops and cannon in reserve. The not so veiled threat was of a bloodbath should any attempt be made to go beyond an orderly demonstration. With this knowledge Jones and O'Connor felt the weight of responsibility bear down on their shoulders. Grey reported that the Chartists perspired and that their faces were pallid. Of course, the prime minister and home secretary were calm.

On 10 April a massive and inspiring gathering was contained, in the face of an impressive display of strength on the part of the state, and passed off as 'one more demonstration'. The expected march on parliament did not take place, on O'Connor's direction, and the petition was treated with contempt in parliament.

Humiliation was mixed with anger within the movement as blame was heaped on the head particularly of O'Connor. Indeed it destroyed him both politically and mentally and he was never to recover in either sense.

The significance of leadership in the events of 1848 must again be grounded in the class structure of British society for anything approaching a 'complete' understanding of what happened. In 1848 Britain was different to the rest of the continent. The industrial landscape of Britain was far more developed than any other country in the world and the working class was larger, more concentrated and more politically developed than anywhere else. In France, for example, the middle class could raise the demand for universal suffrage confident in the knowledge that the working class vote did not represent a significant challenge to their social position. In Britain the enfranchised middle class most definitely viewed the working class, especially in the organised form of Chartism, as a threat. Also, on the continent, the regimes that had fallen had represented the continued official political power of at least some element of the *ancien régime*. The aspiring modern commercial classes of Europe, frustrated at their cowed position under the thumb of aristocratic rule and envious of the industrial advance of Britain, were supporters of the revolutions. In Britain they turned out in uniform to oppose reform.

Only in Belgium could the situation in terms of industrial development be considered to have been anywhere near comparable to Britain. The election of a liberal government the previous year had also paved the way for the enfranchisement of the middle classes. Belgium too was to escape the storm of revolution.

Revolution in Europe hit at a fracture in the social structure between the middle layers of society and the ruling elites. This fracture line was not present in Britain in the same way. A revolution in Britain could not have moved forward only as a political revolution. In order to succeed it would have had to become a social revolution and thus raised the issue of workers' power. The desire for great events was there amongst the working class, and a different leadership—a different *kind* of leadership—could have made a very great difference. But revolution did not occur in Britain, not because workers were less inclined towards it. Indeed the atmosphere in Britain was very similar to that in France at the beginning of the year and the major confrontations and conspiracies which took place over the summer reflected a deep frustration that no breakthrough had been made. It was simply that the idea of social revolution, the overthrow of capitalist property relations and exploitation, was not there in a fully articulated, let alone organised, way.

But it is the impact of the defeat of the Chartists with which we are most concerned. And the impact was earthshaking. On the build up to the Kennington Common gathering it was not just British eyes that were focused on the Chartists. The eyes of Europe were focused on them too—both those who stood on the barricades of Milan and discussed in the workers' clubs of Paris and those key members of the bourgeoisie in the new liberal governments who were waiting for their moment to turn hard against the revolutions and to smash the control that the workers and dispossessed had won in the cities. After the Kennington Common gathering the bourgeoisie of every country and region held in the grip of revolution gained in confidence. It is no coincidence that the 'June days' in Paris, in which workers were massacred, took place after the Chartist retreat. The full significance of what happened in Britain in 1848 must be understood in its European setting. It marked the beginning of the European counter-revolution.

The 10th of April was a defining moment in British history. As the winds of revolution had swept across the continent Britain had stood unmoved. As the wealthy dared to open their eyes and view the unchanged scene before them astonishment passed to near hysterical relief. Church bells rang and prayers of thanks were made. Britain it seemed was different. The British people were temperate and good and the virus of revolution had not been able to cross the Channel. This was the message now rammed home in newspaper editorials, classrooms and from every church pulpit. The myth of a British working class with no revolutionary tradition really begins from this time. The 'Whig' version of British history which put forward a picture of steady constitutional progress towards fairness and decency for all reigned supreme. That epitome of 'Whiggishness', Macaulay, whose first two volumes of his *History of England* came out in 1848, had withdrawn his proofs from the printers after 10 April to give this theme extra emphasis. The volumes met with amazing success, as did the third and fourth volumes five years later. Indeed Macaulay gives us a very neat summary of the idea in his discussion of 'trimming' in relation to one Lord Halifax:

> Everything good, he said, trims between extremes. The temperate zone trims between the climate in which men are roasted and the climate in which they are frozen. The English Church trims between the Anabaptist madness and the Papal lethargy. The English constitution trims between Turkish despotism and Polish anarchy. Virtue is nothing but a just temper between propensities any one of which, if indulged in excess, becomes vice. Nay the perfection of the Supreme Being himself consists in the exact equilibrium of attributes, none of which could preponderate without disturbing the whole moral and physical order of the world.[19]

The confidence of the mid-Victorian ruling class had never stood so high and British ruling class confidence has never stood as high since. Industrially the mightiest nation in the world and reigning supreme abroad and at home—they felt invincible.

Indeed, without too much imagination, we can see in the Great Exhibition of 1851 not only a demonstration of the technological prowess of Britain's industrial capitalists, but also a celebration of domestic power.

It is for all of the above reasons that we cannot play down the significance of 10 April. The motives might be worthy—to rescue the memories of the Chartist leaders perhaps. O'Connor especially took blame in plenty at the time and at the hands of the historians of Chartism. His misfortune in the end was that he led a movement which did not fully understand itself. But we cannot allow such considerations to distract us from a critical understanding of what happened. The British working class *did* have the potential to make revolution in 1848. The events of 10 April *were* highly significant and the *nature* of the leadership *did* make a difference. Revolution did not occur in Britain, not because workers in Britain were essentially, subjectively, less revolutionary, but actually because their potential to make a different kind of revolution than had occured on the continent—a socialist revolution—was greater. Historical consciousness lagged behind objective historical potential.

A very real change came over the working class after the turn of the mid-century. In 1870 Thomas Cooper, reflecting his own personal disillusionment at the decline of the Chartist movement of which he had been a national leader, put it memorably:

> In our old Chartist time, it is true, Lancashire working men were in rags by thousands; and many of them often lacked food. But their intelligence was demonstrated wherever you went. You would see them in groups discussing the great doctrine of political justice... Now, you will see no such groups in Lancashire. But you will hear well dressed working men, talking as they walk with their hands in their pockets, of 'Co-ops'...and their shares in them, or in building societies. And you will see others, like idiots, leading small greyhound dogs, covered with cloth, in a string.[20]

This is harsh. However, it expresses an important truth. Workers in the later decades of the century did not talk class politics in the same way that they had in the 1830s and 1840s. Ever wider layers of workers looked to reformism and by the 1860s this meant looking to the Liberals. Indeed the evidence from poll books suggests that the Tories also were attracting substantial working class support. This is clear in the election results of 1868, after the Second Reform Act where, for the first time, something like an industrial pattern begins to emerge. For the category of 'labourer', for example, probably the most reliably proletarian of the occupational groups recorded, the following results were obtained:

Table of 1868 election results[21]

	Leading Liberal	Leading Tory
Cambridge	214	108
Ipswich	186	160
Rochester	180	116
Sandwich	119	102
Shrewsbury	131	147

It was to take the rise of Labourism towards the end of the century before 'class' became systematically reflected in voting patterns. Until 'class' became institutionalised in politics, election results indicated class consciousness in only the most distorted way and were influenced by all sorts of other factors—often, for example, the party allegiance of the most hated local capitalist.

It was support for the Liberals, however, that must be seen as the most significant development in terms of the rise of a more politically moderate working class and a reformist consciousness. Probably the clearest symbol of this shift was Ernest Jones, to the despair of Marx and Engels, standing as a Liberal in the 1868 election. His funeral the following year was symbolic too, attended by 80,000 mourners, mainly working class, and led by figures from the Liberal establishment. It was in this period that Engels wrote to Marx of the English proletariat having disgraced itself and a little earlier that Britain, 'this most bourgeois of all nations, is apparently aiming ultimately at the possession of a bourgeois aristocracy and a bourgeois proletariat as well as a bourgeoisie'.[22]

In fact the bourgeoisie never completely dominated or 'captured' the thinking of workers in this period and 'class' was always present both objectively and in social experience and consciousness. Strikes, for example, pepper the entire period, including strikes by gas workers, match girls and dockers in the late 1880s and early 1890s. The mass of workers still lived in dire

121

poverty and reforms, when they came, still had to be fought for. Even the best paid workers and their trade union leaders were aware of where the lines of class were drawn. Hobsbawm puts it well:

> The labour aristocrat might wear a top hat and think on business matters exactly like his employer, but when the pickets were out against the boss, he knew what to do. Moreover, he developed, if on a narrow basis, a solidarity and class consciousness, a belief that so long as a man worked for his wages his interests were exclusively dominated by that fact.[23]

There were moments also when this awareness of class achieved high political and internationalist expression. Most inspiring of all were the early May Days of 1890, 1891 and 1892 which saw truly mass gatherings of up to 300,000 and which marked the dawn after a long dark night for socialist politics in Britain.

But we cannot explain or fully appreciate the significance of that dawn without also explaining why it took so long in coming and why it was that the militant working class consciousness of the 1840s disappeared.

Again only a materialist analysis based on class can adequately explain this change and again it must be emphasised that Marxism does not rely on a reduction to economics for its understanding of history. We cannot straightforwardly say that after 1850 there was an upswing in trade and that therefore the Chartist movement went into decline as a new trade union and reformist consciousness replaced it. For the Webbs, for example, this notion of an absolute break, before and after 1850, allowed them to portray Chartism as a dangerous, if colourful, aberration before the rise of the 'proper' modern trade union movement. On this view the end of Chartism has nothing to do with the later movement.

It is true that a major expansion of economic activity did occur during the 1850s, especially in the dominant cotton industry. The number of workers employed in the mills increased from 540,000 in 1844 to 646,000 in 1859.[24] Wages also rose on average over the decade. But real care must be taken in here in interpretation. At the very beginning of the decade wage depression had occurred and compared with average wages in 1839 the increase by 1850 was modest.[25] Throughout most of the 1850s wages were fairly stationary. Where improvements did occur struggle was still needed to push up wage levels—as in the 1853-54 strikes which led to a brief recovery of Chartism. Even then employers were quick to claw back their concessions. Only after 1858 can a general improvement be said to have occurred. Indeed there are so many empirical factors to be taken into account here that it is beyond the scope of this article to give an adequate treatment. Periods of price inflation, real family income, spells of unemployment, wage differentials, housing, health, sanitation and so on must all be included in such an analysis. Suffice to say that the improvements which did occur for workers during the period cannot be considered to have been so substantial as to have provided the basis of the end of the Chartist movement.

We must also remember that although the Chartist movement was past its former glories, certainly after the summer of 1848, it limped on with attempts at revival well into the 1850s. It was only formally wound up in 1860. We cannot, then, crudely point to economic factors in order to explain the decline of working class radicalism in the 1850s. We must understand it rather in the context of historic defeat in combination with a generalised expansion of industry.[26] The ranks of the impoverished artisans were declining at a pace and the workers of the new factory proletariat, though growing in numbers, no longer saw in themselves a generalised alternative to the system.

In the mid-1970s Stedman Jones put forward a largely structuralist account of the period after 1850 in which a 'new stage of industrialisation' imposed a settlement of a now unchallengeable capitalism.[27] The subjective experiences of the working classwere, however, marginalised and the resulting picture was one sided and partial. Fleeting references aside, the significance of 1848 as a break in the generalised experience of the working class was missed, and the way was clear for a view of an unbroken working class subjectivity—the 'continuity' of the working class Radical tradition. Building on this framework the 'pre-postmodern' Joyce described the emergence of a deferential cotton proletariat in the last third of the 19th century.[28] In Joyce's account, the supreme confidence of the capitalist class was mirrored by a sense of vulnerability on the part of mill workers who responded to employers' growing paternalism with an obsequious loyalty. Class conflict was written out of the picture and the whole process smoothed out as a continuous phenomenon. With class struggle edited out of the story the way was clear for

123

Joyce to move towards an account of consciousness which dispenses with 'class' altogether, and with it the 'economic' as an explanatory factor in history. Economism collapsed into idealism.

This is not to say that economic factors are not relevant to an understanding of the social history of the era of Victorian Reform. The very real improvements in wages and real earnings for large numbers of workers in the 1860s, for example, clearly had an effect on their outlook. It is true that the late 1870s saw the beginning of a long and uneven depression but one in which a decline of prices for basic goods, as well as the mass import of cheap consumables from the empire, offset the effects for workers.[29] However, this does not really explain the shift towards liberalism in the working class. It is conceivable that such economic factors, especially in the 1860s, might have restored the confidence of workers and led to a recovery in the militancy of the 1840s. They did not, and to achieve a fuller understanding other factors would have to be built into the picture.

Again it is not the intention of this article to attempt anything like a complete account of the social history of the working class in the second half of the 19th century. But certainly we would have to consider the seeming vindication of the bourgeois world view after the revolutions of 1848 had passed, the apparent permanence of the ever expanding industrial system, the preparedness of a confident bourgoise to concede reform, and the growing awareness on the part of the ruling class of the need to construct a more developed and stable capitalist social order and to grant a place within this for the working class. It did now seem that economic improvement could be achieved without dramatic political change.

Within the working class we would need to look at the rise of a conservative and privileged trade union bureaucracy, the apparent effectiveness of trade union bargaining, the rise of a pro-capitalist working class press, the reconstruction of the working class family, the growth and near institutionalisation of anti-Irish racism and the detachment of industrial struggle from a wider social vision.

Strands of history from below here mix and intertwine with strands of history from above. The process was not inevitable but it happened. The key fact, however, is that it was all consistent with, indeed demands, a materialist account of history. And certainly concepts of the economic, of class and of class struggle itself, despite Joyce's attempt to elide them from the story, were a constant theme.

124

By stressing continuities in history, focusing solely on language and dismissing the 'material' and class, the postmodernists ignore the real, actual history that working class people lived through these decades. They cannot explain the end of Chartism and the slide into working class liberalism. For them it is all the same thing. But, more than this, they cannot explain the end of working class Liberalism either. The long period of working class political conservatism, which began in the 1850s, lasted, with the exception of the New Unionism of the early 1890s, up until the years before the First World War. This period came crashing to an end with the shock of the Great Unrest which began in 1910 and which was only cut short by the war itself. What is significant for us is that those sections of workers who began the revolt were the same workers who had been the very pillars of working class respectability. To the bewilderment of their employers as well as to their Liberal trade union leaders, who now found that their powers of persuasion and calm negotiation were reduced to nothing, these workers and others staged wave after wave of militant lightning strikes which shook not only the industrial districts but the whole of the country. These workers—the Northumberland miners, the north eastern railwaymen—who had once been seen as the archetypal 'aristocrats' of labour now began to throw up picket lines over the most apparently insignificant workplace issues and take an active interest in the ideas of the revolutionary syndicalists:

> The miners of Northumberland and Durham were the 'aristocrats' of the industry, they had been the last to join the Miners' Federation, they were proud and aloof: and it seemed almost incredible that they should be behaving with such an unreasoned, such a bitter vehemence. Was there something, perhaps, behind all this which did not meet the eye?[30]

There was indeed. There was the experience of price rises for consumables caused by economic inflation following the influx of South African gold. Life was getting harder materially. But there was more, much more, than this. These workers were sick and tired of being taken for fools. They and their fathers and mothers had never forgotten that they were workers, not for an instant. For a long time they had had little faith in their ability to change their society. But they had always been clear that their employers were wealthy and that they were not, and that these two facts were related. They had now chosen to reject their previous compliant behaviour towards their capitalist lords and to assert the power and strength that they had always suspected they might possess.[31] Such things the postmodernists will never understand.

The distortions which run through postmodernist histories stem from their underlying methodological assumptions. The rejection of a material basis to historical analysis and an exclusive reliance on language lead to empirical shallowness and an inability to properly answer the questions thrown up by historical events.

History and language

Key to the 'linguistic turn' of the postmodernists is the claim that only by looking at what people said about themselves at the time can we comment on history. But to what extent can we rely on how people expressed themselves to really understand what was going on? Is it the case that people's own ideas about the significance of what they were doing, and the traditions on which they drew to talk about their movements, are always the best guide to the truth? To what extent are we entitled to say more than they said about themselves? The questions here go to the heart of the methods of the 'linguistic turn' and must also involve discussions of ideology and historical consciousness.

Is it always the case that the actors of history speak openly and plainly of their actions and intentions? Christopher Hill in his book *A Nation of Change and Novelty* suggests not. Apart from those situations when half truths are told for reasons of circumspection or to avoid incrimination and the eye of the authorities, there are many ways in which words do not convey the full meaning of what is being said, or even say the opposite of what is meant. Hill gives us the example of the parliamentary MPs shortly before the outbreak of the English Civil War. Through a combination of unwillingness to criticise the king and lack of clarity about the depth of the social crisis that was carrying them forward the MPs reserved their scorn for the king's advisers and the court establishment. Charles I himself was always praised and the crucial issue of the monarch's 'prerogative' to raise taxes skirted around:

> 'Even in 1628', Sir Geoffrey Elton insists, 'the opposition leadership carefully avoided any proposals which could be read as an

invasion of prerogative rights'… But verbal caution should not be equated with acquiescence. The wholly conventional nature of the distinction between the king and his advisers was assumed on all sides… Sir Edward Phelips spoke of 'the original contract between king and people', and Sir Nathaniel Rich noted that some said 'this House hath no good opinion of monarchical government. 'Tis false' he added.[32]

These men would not have seen at this time that their opposition to the court would lead to the beheading of Charles I. This is not a trivial example. The ambiguities of statements by the Parliamentarians have long been used by anti-Marxist historians to deny the class nature of the English Civil War. Such interpretations only hold up for as long as we stay at the surface of events. Only when we look behind 'the word' and appreciate the social and political context in which historical utterances are made do their meanings become clear.

When we look at the origins of the Charter, the 'six points' around which Chartism was organised, the need to see beyond the 'texts' again becomes clear. On the one hand it is true that the Charter was essentially a manifesto of political reform and in this sense, on a purely literal interpretation, has its roots in the Radical tradition. On the other hand the Charter itself did not really represent the extent and depth of the Chartist movement in some very important senses.

The early Chartist leadership, certainly judged against the later history of the movement, were moderates. Individuals such as William Lovett and Francis Place of the London Working Men's Association had a key influence at the time of the drafting of the Charter (although they were later to squabble over its authorship). Place in particular was in close communication with the half dozen 'Radical' MPs in parliament. These figures did see themselves as standing in the long tradition of political reform. But this was not a tradition which could be said to encompass the later movement—the demands of the 1842 general strike, the frequent expressions of social discontent, the stubborn rejection of alliances with the middle class and the socialist politics of the later leaderships. Demands such as the abolition of the monarchy and of the House of Lords and for female suffrage, which were widespread within the working class, were excluded from the Charter. This gap between the Radicals in parliament (the 'sham

127

radicals' as O'Brien called them) and the mass of the growing movement was a source of friction within the LWMA and the motives of those involved were conflicting. Indeed for Francis Place the Charter seemed to provide a means by which dangerous agitation against the hated Poor Laws could be channelled in a harmless direction:

> The Bill which was to be presented to Parliament by the Radical MPs, now had to be got together by the Working Men's Association, and Lovett was charged with the drafting of it. After meeting the Radicals, he made the alterations they suggested and took it to Francis Place. Place agreed to help but insisted as a condition that the London Working Men's Association 'would take no further cognisance of the Poor Law.' To which they seem to have agreed.[33]

The social grievances which drove the Chartist movement forward did begin to be included in the appendices of the second and third versions of the Charter. A brief glance at the pages of the *Northern Star* makes it clear that the social condition of the working class was a constant and ever present concern. A narrow and literal reading of the Charter cannot then be taken as evidence that Chartism was purely political, as opposed to being a political *and* social movement with an economic base. The working class of the 1830s and 1840s made the Charter the focus of the accumulated resentments of the previous 20 years. It was not, however, a direct or all encompassing expression of the mood of the working class during those years.

The question of how history is recorded as well as who writes the texts of history, both at the time of historically significant periods and after they have passed, clearly means that we cannot take a naive and uncritical reading of them as a literal guide to historical truth.[34]

But there are deeper reasons why the consciousness of the agents of history needs to be interpreted in its broad historical setting from the vantage point of the present. Firstly, it is true that social struggle is expressed in the contemporary ideas of the time—in the language available. And more than this, the terms of that language can be shared by both the oppressed and their oppressors. And yet clearly the meanings of those terms are different. A good example is the uses to which the Bible has been put and the ways in which the meanings of biblical reference have been contested.

Wycliffe's English translation of the Bible and, more directly, John Ball's interpretation was a crucial ideological yeast in the period of the English Peasants' Revolt of the late 14th century. In Germany in the 1620s peasant movements fought against their landlord rulers under the banner of Lutheran doctrines of the New Testament. As Engels wrote, commenting on the treatment given to the Peasant Wars of 1525 by German historians:

> The German ideology still sees nothing except violent theological bickering in the struggles that ended the Middle Ages. Should the people of that time, say our home bred historians and sages, have only come to an understanding concerning celestial things, there would have been no ground whatever to quarrel over earthly things. These ideologists are gullible enough to accept unquestioningly all the illusions that an epoch makes about itself... They have hardly any idea to this day of the class struggles which were fought out in these upheavals, and of which the political slogan on the banner is every time a bare expression...
>
> Even the so-called religious wars of the 16th century involved positive material class interests; those wars were class wars too, just as the later internal collisions in France. Although the class struggles of that day were clothed in religious shibboleths, and though the interests, requirements, and demands of the various classes were concealed behind a religious screen, this changed nothing in the matter, and is easily explained by the conditions of the time.[35]

What is not being argued here is that religion was a mere wrapping for otherwise developed secular ideas. Religious ideas of course express religious feelings. The point is that expressions of religious protest had a social significance and originated either in material distress or in political frustration. The degree to which this was understood at the time also varied in terms of the social location of those involved. In the towns opposition to ecclesiastical authority was much more consciously political. For the peasants in the huge rural expanses of late medieval Germany, influenced by ideas of peasant communism and the Anabaptists, religion expressed as yet unrealisable utopian yearnings. We could make similar points about the religious conflicts of the English Civil War or even of the religious influences within the working class of the 19th century before they were largely displaced by the rise of secular socialist politics and a developed reformist labour movement.

We have to be aware then in our reading of history that tensions exist within ideologies and that historical consciousness can be contradictory. The same words and general language can have very different meanings and concepts behind them both to different social groups and at different periods in history. The term 'democracy' for example, has proved to be extraordinarily elastic in its usage. In the 19th century it was anathema to liberal and Tory alike, with connotations not too far away from anarchy. Today it is a key part of the ideological toolchest of Western imperialism used to justify the most ferociously anti-democratic actions around the world. Equally, of course, it is a central part of the socialist argument for a society based on political and economic equality and justice. In 1989, during the Eastern European Revolutions, democracy meant different things to different groups in society. For entrepreneurs it meant the freedom to trade, for students intellectual freedom, for journalists and artists freedom of expression, for workers the right to bargain with employers, to be members of free trade unions and the right to strike. What has happened since is, of course, a different story. But the fact remains that behind a single word multi-layered meanings can exist. Language, and the way it expresses historical experience, must be read carefully.

It is also the case that, in the absence of ideas which directly express the forward movement of historical events, the language and symbols of previous epochs become used once again. Town speakers in the 1989 Eastern European movements quoted Voltaire and the ideals of the French Revolution of 1789. On the mass assemblies and processions of the Chartist years the Caps of Liberty and cockades of the French Republic also appeared. Frequently in history events and actions run ahead of the language available to express them. The mass strikes of 1918 in Germany threw up workers' and soldiers' councils which went on to pose the question of political power during the revolutionary months of 1919. Yet these same councils, in the absence of alternatives, elected right wing social democratic figures into positions of political influence. This gap between action and language is not just of historical interest. It makes a real difference to the outcome of events. It is a political problem. As Marx famously put it:

> The tradition of all dead generations weighs like a nightmare on the brain of the living. And just when they seem engaged in revolutionising themselves and things, in creating something that has

never existed, precisely in such periods of revolutionary crisis they anxiously conjure up spirits of the past to their service and borrow from them names, battle cries, and costumes in order to present the new scene of world history in this time honoured guise and this borrowed language.[36]

The postmodernists' stress on continuities—one of the consequences of the 'linguistic turn'—means that they are also unable to explain the ways in which perceptions of class changed throughout the 19th century. In language the feudal expressions of social status which were still being used gave way to the language of class:

> The political debate which followed the death of Palmerston in 1865 and ended with the passing of the Second Reform Bill two years later led to a revival of interest in the problems and terminology of 'class'. It was the change in the economic circumstances in the 1870s and 1880s, however, and the disturbance of the mid-Victorian social balance which shifted the debate onto a wider front... Whatever may be said of the new phase, one development is incontrovertible. The language of 'ranks', 'orders', and 'degrees', which...survived the Industrial Revolution, was finally cast into limbo. The language of class, like the facts of class, remained.[37]

These changes reflected objective realities in society, indeed would not have been possible without them. Similarly the character and forms of struggle in widely differing epochs must reflect something of the social structures which underlie them. In feudal times, for example, the relationship between the tenant and the Lord of the Manor was one of servitude and patronage. It was a particular relationship in a tightly defined social sphere. The relationship also was experienced as a vertical and familial one of duties and obligations. In capitalism the relationship between a worker and a capitalist was general. Any worker could, in principle, work for any capitalist. This meant that the natural affinities felt by a worker were more likely to be towards other workers than towards an individual capitalist. This set of productive relations made possible a generalised working class consciousness which had never been possible before. This, in turn, was expressed both in social and economic movements of the working class and in language. The general unionism of 1834, for example, in which year the Grand National Consolidated Trades Union exploded into life to reach a membership of almost 800,000 before declining again before the end of the year, was only possible because of the long term economic shift towards the factory system. These changes also gave rise to the phenomenon of the working class activist who could sustain their commitment and involvment through the peaks and troughs of working class struggle. Armed with more or less developed ideologies of the historical significance of the working class, people such as William Cobbett, Francis Place, William Benbow and James Bronterre O'Brien began to shape the outlook and thinking of their movements. It was such figures also, and others like them, who began to sketch out, albeit in faint and partial terms, the first notions of a way past the horrors of early 19th century capitalism which were based on the working class.

In the end it is this aspect of class struggle in history which shapes the ways in which we approach and interpret it. It is what connects the present with the past and what makes history a living thing from which we can learn in order to better equip us in the struggle today.

CHAPTER 7

Myth and reality in British working class struggle

Chris Bambery

This essay looks at the development of British working class politics from the close of the Chartist period through to the emergence of the Independent Labour Party. It does not rehearse the argument about the supposed 'aristocratic hegemony' over British society in the 19th century. Suffice it to say that the approach here agrees with Marx that, while often aristocratic in form, control of the state was thoroughly bourgeois in content. The main aim here is to examine Perry Anderson's argument about the development of the British working class which, he claims, was fundamentally weaker than its European counterparts.

In 'Origins of the Present Crisis' Anderson argues regarding British working class development up to the middle of the 19th century that:

> It achieved no victories, but its defeats were astonishing. In 1819 it organised the first national political campaign of the post-war period, so scaring to both the bourgeoisie and aristocracy that it provoked a massacre and exceptional legislation. In 1831-32 it formed the great heaving swell of the Reform Movement, constantly threatening to capsize the bourgeois groupings adroitly navigating on its surface. From 1829-34 it produced in Owenism the first, mass socialist movement of the century. When this was crushed in 1836, it rose again in an independent working class movement for reform: Chartism, its final supreme effort, lasted for a decade. Wrecked by its pitifully weak leadership and strategy,

in the end it collapsed without a fight. With it disappeared for 30 years the élan and combativity of the class. A profound caesura in English working class history supervened.[1]

Warming to this theme he adds:

The shattering fiasco of Chartism finally broke the morale of the early proletariat; a period of intense shock and retreat followed. For 30 years of prolonged catatonic withdrawal, the most insurgent working class in Europe became the most numbed and docile.[2]

This earth shattering defeat, Anderson argues, shaped the British working class of the 20th century:

It was not until the 1880s that the working class really began to recover from the traumatic defeat of the 1840s. By then the world had moved on. In consciousness and combativity, the English working class had been overtaken by almost all its continental opposites. Marxism had missed it.[3]

In his 1984 preface to *Outcast London* Gareth Stedman Jones takes up this argument and argues that there were three developments in the second half of the 19th century peculiar to Britain. Firstly, the dominant tradition in the intelligentsia was one of compliance and conformism. Secondly, as a consequence of this, Britain was marked by not having a mass working class party with 'revolutionary ambition' (the two points are linked). Lastly, this led to the triumph of Labourism.[4] Stedman Jones further argues that the second half of the 19th century saw 'the triumph of liberal ideas and assumptions among the mass of the population'.[5]

In contrast to these arguments I wish to cast doubt on how far Gladstonian liberalism penetrated the British working class—I am not sure whether Anderson's use of the term English is a slip or implies that Scottish and Welsh workers escaped this process—and I want to claim that as early as the 1860s there is strong evidence of the pressures which would finally blow the Liberal Party apart as the premier party of British capital.

In arguing this there can be no question that 1848 and the defeat of Chartism does represent a fundamental break. At its height, in the 'Sacred Month' of 1839 and with the 1842 general strike, there was a unification of political demands for universal suffrage with economic demands. This combination of politics and economics gave Chartism its revolutionary potential. In those years the British working class invented mass and flying pickets and the general strike. That is why Marx and Engels argued in *The German Ideology* that 'even a minority of workers who combine and go on strike, very soon find themselves compelled to act in a revolutionary way'.[6]

In the late 1830s and in the 1840s British trade unions were a very real threat to British capitalism. By the 1850s and the 1860s they were not. As a consequence of that Marx and Engels radically revised their view on the possibilities of trade unionism challenging capital.

Of course the conditions which the British working class was operating in were radically different from their neighbours. In Britain the bourgeois revolution was complete. The French, Italian and German working classes were shaped by the revolutions of 1848 against autocracy, the Irish working class by rural insurgency against the colonial ascendancy. This gave them a more direct, insurrectionary tradition, although this can be exaggerated.

Marx understood 1848-49 was a turning point. That is why he withdrew from active politics for a period. But when Marx looked at the British working class, he connected its defeat with that of the European revolutions. The two things were not sealed off from each other. A letter to the *Beehive* in September 1864 remarked that the July Revolution of 1830 in France helped precipitate both the Polish uprising of 1831 and the movement which won the 1832 Reform Act in Britain. The National Union of the Working Classes and Others, which included Bronterre O'Brien, Henry Hetherington and William Lovett, was founded in 1831 in response to the French, Belgian and Polish revolutions. Harney made contact with Engels after he had carried the latter's reports from Germany in the *Northern Star*. The Fraternal Democrats were founded in 1846 at Harney's initiative and organised solidarity with the Cracow Uprising and protests against the threat of war with the US over the ownership of Oregon, under the slogan, 'No vote, no musket'.

Marx in his 'Inaugural Address' to the First International points to the defeat of the European revolutions of 1848-49 as being a turning point for the British working class. He argued that it 'unmanned the English working classes and broke the faith in

135

their own cause'.[7] But he also pointed to the Ten Hour Bill of 1847, the rise of the cooperative movement and the riot over Sunday trading as evidence that the British working class was not crushed. It is worth recalling that even in the 1850s the left wing *Reynolds Weekly* sold 50,000 copies.

The year 1850 is a convenient date with which to mark a major shift in British capitalism. With the railway boom British capitalism regained its confidence and began its further expansion to become the workshop of the world. On the back of this boom the British ruling class could move from a policy of coercion to a policy of containing and absorbing working class politics—or, to be more precise, the skilled working class. Economic expansion made it possible to grant reforms like the ten hour day and the Factory Acts, and sections of the leadership of the craft unions were brought into the orbit of Liberal Party politics.

The working class itself went through a significant change in the second half of the 19th century. In 1851 the largest category of employment remained agriculture with 1.5 million workers; next came domestic service with 1 million workers; then construction with 700,000. Cotton employed 500,000 workers who largely lived in the classic mill towns where housing clustered round the place of work. Another 500,000 were employed in other sectors of the textile industry, many still working from home. Clothing and footwear employed another 750,000, many again working from home or in small workshops. Woodworking (160,000) and printing (80,000) were still workshop based and largely unmechanised.[8]

Six million jobs were created between 1841 and 1911, 52 percent in services and construction—it was never the case that the majority of British workers were employed in the manufacturing sector. Mechanisation meant newer pits could be dug with better ventillation and drainage. The number of miners grew from 400,000 to 1 million. Engineering grew to employ 570,000 workers who provided much of the world's steam engines and locomotives. Large factories and shipyards appeared—though still reliant on individual craft workers like fitters and millwrights rather than machines.

Radical changes took place in the methods of production. Wool, carpet making and some parts of the clothing industry moved almost entirely to factory production. New science based industries like chemicals and electrical engineering appeared.

By the end of the century machine tools had begun to replace fitters who previously had built steam engines by hand filing metal casings. There was also a massive increase in what is termed the service sector and in the production of consumer goods. Britain was the first industrial nation but it also created the first consumer society. And many jobs were created in manufacturing industries serving consumer needs—paper, printing and publishing, timber, furniture and clothing.[9]

The shift to full factory production meant that weavers saw their livelihoods lost. The vast majority of them suffered immiseration and were forced to find new employment. A minority became small businessmen and employers. It would be interesting to find out just who were the former Chartists who in 1885 gathered in Halifax, as Edward Thompson tells us, to toast Gladstone with lemonade. Into which category did they fall?[10] In a period of economic expansion and of general improvement in working class conditions skilled workers could see the possibility of advance by both parliamentary reform and narrow, sectional, union self organisation.

But it is also important to remember that the 1850s and 1860s still saw that classic protest of the disenfranchised, the bread riot, which London's East End experienced in 1855, 1861 and 1869.[11] Skilled unions might have been formally ready to denounce strikes in their PR type representations to royal commissions but they were still ready to take industrial action. Neither were the 1850s and 1860s free of class struggle, with an engineering lockout in 1851 and a series of major strikes in the 1860s. The radical impulse in British working class politics was not dead and revived significantly in the 1860s.

The figure most identified with the period is undoubtedly the 'labour aristocrat'. If the term has any meaning it describes a skilled worker—typically an engineer—who still had a degree of control over the productive process. Machine builders in this period did not, by and large, follow blueprints but were employed to handmake the machines. These skilled workers owned their own tools and might even employ labourers. But to offset this we have to remember that skilled workers had to go through periods of layoff, of short time working and of intervals between jobs often involving them in travel to another town or city. The seemingly good wages earned by skilled workers in the shipyard do not look so good when the calculation moves from the weekly rate to just how many full weeks were worked in a year.

137

The motivation of British trade unionists in launching the First International is often portrayed as a simple desire to stop the importation of foreign scabs. There was rather more to it than that. The 1860s saw a revival of working class struggle in both Britain and France. The struggle of London building workers for a nine hour day led to the formation of the London Trades Council in 1860 and the launch of a new, radical paper, the *Beehive,* the next year. This new movement responded warmly to the fight for the unification of Italy, renewed rebellion in Poland and rallied to the side of the Northern states in the American Civil War.

In 1864 Garibaldi's welcome in London was so large—it took six hours to travel from Nine Elms to St James—and so obviously working class, with a great display of trade union banners, that the government cut short his visit. The Working Men's Garibaldi Committee called a protest meeting at Primrose Hill which was broken up by police.[12] Working class support for the Northern states in the US flourished after Lincoln abolished slavery. After one trade union meeting of 3,000 in solidarity with the North, *The Times* declared:

> The members of the trades' unions would have a natural bias towards the North, other classes have insensibly acquired a leaning towards the South.[13]

The US historian James McPherson has, in *Drawn With the Sword,* linked the American Civil War and the North's victory with the renewed agitation which led to the passing of the 1867 Reform Act.[14] Collins and Abramsky point out that there was an element of class polarisation in this:

> The Italian cause had friends in every section of society; the Northern states gradually won the sympathy of radical and labour movements; while enthusiastic support for Poland was almost confined to the working class.[15]

This was the background to the launch of the First International and to Marx's involvement in it (despite Engels' initial scepticism). The wish by British trade unionists to use that body to prevent the importation of foreign scabs is half the story. There was, in fact, a very fruitful two way relationship.

The First International was the first political body in which trade unions participated as affiliated bodies. It initiated the campaign for the eight hour day, which later would become the rallying point for the New Unionism, and it ensured that British unions participated in a number of its international campaigns. In turn the British unions ensured through their votes in the First International Marx's victory over Proudhon, its support for the eight hour day, support for land nationalisation and for the whole concept of workers involving themselves in political activity.

The Reform League was formed in April 1865 by middle class radicals and a number of working class leaders (including two members of the First International's general council, Odger and Eccarius). This revived the campaign for universal male suffrage and the First International played a role in ensuring support for the Radical League.

There were some massive demonstrations in the 1860s. One in 1866 saw workers defy a government ban on their using Hyde Park (then the preserve of the rich) by tearing up the railings in a major riot:

> On 23 July a huge protest demonstration was called in Hyde Park, to forestall which Sir Richard Mayne, the commissioner of police, declared the meeting illegal and the cabinet ordered the park gates closed. The angry demonstrators in their thousands stormed the park in the Bayswater Road. Despite the massive presence of police and troops they tore up a hundred yards of the iron railings near to Marble Arch, and then, under the provocation of police brutality, proceeded to tear up the rest as far as Hyde Park Corner.[16]

The next year 150,000 workers, led by a red flag with the cap of liberty, successfully defied a government ban on their demonstration. There followed massive demonstrations against the public hanging of three Fenians, the 'Manchester Martyrs'.

Two years later, as Tory repression mounted in Ireland, 100,000 people people demonstrated for the release of Irish Republican prisoners. Marx remarked:

> The main feature of the demonstration had been ignored. It was that at least part of the English working class lost their prejudice against the Irish.[17]

The revival of working class self activity in the 1860s centred around strikes, internationalism and the franchise.

We should remember that while Marx pointed out in the 1870s that 'the organisation of the working class through the trade unions had acquired a degree of universality', he also added that they were totally lacking in the spirit of generalisation and revolutionary ardour.[18]

British trade unions were very much shaped by these years. They were still of course largely craft unions concerned with protecting their status and attempting to control the labour market. They were not apolitical. They were pro-Liberal. But above all they were sectional, built not across industries but across trades, and they accepted the division between politics (parliamentary activity) and economics (trade union activity).

Even by the 1860s, however, strains were showing in their alliance with the Liberals. Industrial disputes were often brutal. Troops were used against London building workers in 1860; in 1862 the Admiralty sacked workers on strike at Chatham dockyard; in 1866 there were the 'Sheffield Outrages' as pickets attacked scabs; and in 1869 five striking miners were shot dead in Denbighshire.

The 1870s saw further tensions on the industrial front which strained the unions' alignment with the Liberals. The year 1871 saw the nine hours movement among the engineers and a three month long coal strike in South Wales; in 1872 the courts were used to stop a strike by London gas workers; and from 1872 to 1874 there was the spectacular rise of Joseph Arch's National Agricultural Labourers' Union. A growing number of newly formed trades councils began to discuss standing independent labour candidates. This spurt of activity was a forerunner of the unemployed agitation of 1886-87 and the New Unionism. Again, it was also connected to a revival of struggle in Europe and to the rise of the Paris Commune.

The events of the late 1880s and 1890s are more familiar. The unemployed riot in London's West End in 1886 was followed by the subsequent free speech fight which culminated in Bloody Sunday the next year. The socialists of the SDF and of William Morris's Socialist League attracted a real audience (although their sectarian attitude to trade union struggle meant they could not capitalise on it).

A brief economic upturn in 1888 led to an increase in strikes with 509 officially recorded (320 for wage increases). The Bryant and May match workers strike in July 1888 marks the beginning of the New Unionism involving, as it did, unskilled women workers many of whom were Irish (and many of them living in what was called the 'Fenian Barracks' in Bow). The East End of London was rocked by the unionisation of the gas workers and by the docks strike of 1889. Socialists like Eleanor Marx, Ben Tillett, John Burns and Tom Mann played a vital role. Again the involvement of Irish workers was noticable. In 1890 London's first May Day rally drew 350,000 people, while 10,000 marked it in Northampton and 6,000 in Leeds.

An employers' offensive began to take shape in response. British capitalism was already aware it was losing ground to the US and Germany. The growing internationalisation of capital (which was the dominant feature of imperialism) meant British capital had to close the gap in terms of both productivity and profitability. The Conservative Party was reforged as industrialists and businessmen joined it and it began to demonstrate its pro-imperialism through its opposition to Irish 'Home Rule'. Following the US, employers' organisations like the Engineering Employers' Federation were also created which tried to emulate the tactics of US union busters like Carnegie, Gould, Morgan and the other 'Robber Barons'.

As the employers gained successes, greater political generalisation was created in the working class. Previously socialists had been key activists. Now they began to find they could attract support for their political ideas. This was the case in Bradford with the 1890-91 Manningham Mills strike. Socialists like Tom Maguire could attack the Liberal mill owners, who backed the Tory owner of the mill, and the Liberal councillors who banned strike support meetings, unleashed the police and had the Riot Act read. And these calls found an echo. Similarly when socialists attacked the police and the evils of big business they attracted attention.

But this politicisation was not accompanied by an increase in the feeling of common, class strength. The defeat of the strike meant workers were won to the idea of an eight hour day but now saw it as coming through parliament rather than through their own self activity.

The Independent Labour Party was formed in Bradford out of the Manningham Mills strike. The ILP grew most quickly in the West Riding where links with the Liberals had been eroded, in the West of Scotland where the strength of the Liberals had prevented even the election of Lib-Lab MPs (as Keir Hardie discovered), South Wales where the pro-Liberal leadership of the

South Wales Miners' Federation was already under attack from the rank and file and from Lancashire where the Tories were strong and the Liberals weak. A further legal offensive against the unions eventually forced the trade unions to break with the Liberals and to join in launching the Labour Representation Committee (the precursor to today's Labour Party).

Why was the Labour Party to emerge free of what Stedman Jones termed 'revolutionary ambition'? It did not have a formal commitment to socialism. And it certainly did not have the commitment to Marxism of its European counterparts—though we should remember that that commitment largely remained on paper.

British circumstances were different. The Labour Party did not have to go through the repression the German SPD experienced and so did not have to construct 'the state within the state' which so characterised German social democracy. And in Britain the trade unions created a mass working class party rather than the other way round as in Europe. But to all this we must add the inability of British socialists to help shape either the Independent Labour Party or the Labour Representation Committee. Rather than follow Engels' advice to throw themselves into this real movement of workers, they maintained a sectarian stance.

The 1850s and 1860s were the exceptional period in the history of British capitalism, when Britain was truly the 'Workshop of the World'. But it was to prove a brief period of supremacy. By the 1870s it had been overtaken industrially by the US and in the 1890s by Germany. It would be a mistake to draw an analogy between the years following the defeat of Chartism and, say, the downturn in struggle which set in in Britain from 1976 onwards. The 1850s and 1860s saw increasing prosperity for British workers in which union organisation stabilised. For skilled workers the experience was one of a reduction in hours, a Saturday afternoon free from work, an improvement in housing and in general lifestyle. None of that kind of progress applied to the Thatcher years in Britain.

The immediate legacy of the emergence of the trade unions in the 1850s and 1860s was one of sectionalism and of the separation of economics and politics. But by the 1880s Britain had moved back into synchronisation with the European working class. In contrast to the Anderson/Stedman Jones picture, the development of the British working class was marked from New

Unionism onwards by a series of sudden sharp explosions of struggle (the Great Unrest, the First Shop Stewards' Movement, the strikes of the 1930s and the upsurge of 1972-74). In those struggles it was possible to see how sectionalism could break down and socialist politics could find a ready audience.

Associated with these events were the repeated attempts of the ruling class to launch an employers' offensive to close the ever widening gap with their rivals. This offensive centred more and more on using the state with legal attacks on the unions and, under Thatcher, the direct use of the police and courts.

At the beginning of this century certain areas of Britain experienced rapid industrialisation and immigration, creating social upheaval and radicalisation rivalled perhaps not by Petrograd, Barcelona or Turin but certainly Berlin. Here I am thinking not just of Clydeside and South Wales but of Sheffield and Coventry. Again Marxist politics, far from being an alien force, could find a ready audience.

Sectionalism also created shop stewards' organisation. For the Marxist tradition this is important because we can see a tendency at high points of struggle for shop stewards' organisation to grow over into a shop stewards' movement capable of acting independently of the bureaucracy and the Labour Party. This in turn creates the potential for new, rank and file forms of working class democracy.

143

CHAPTER 8

The Communist Party Historians' Group

Sam Ashman

The names of those who were either members of, or associated with, the Historians' Group of the British Communist Party (CP) in the years following the Second World War are those of some of the most important historians of this century. They have been crucial to development of Marxist historiography, and to the development of history in each of their respective fields and have acted as pioneers of 'history from below', the rewriting of history from the standpoint of the oppressed and the exploited.

Just to name the individuals involved is to demonstrate the group's importance. Among its members were Christopher Hill, for many years the dominant figure in the history of the 17th century who shaped a generation of students of the English Revolution, E P Thompson, who wrote, amongst other things, the pathbreaking *The Making of the English Working Class*; and Eric Hobsbawm, the author of the important trilogy on the history of the 'long 19th century'—from the French Revolution of 1789 to the First World War, *The Age of Revolution*, *The Age of Capital* and *The Age of Empire*. There was also Maurice Dobb whose book *Studies in the Development of Capitalism* was both a crucial influence on the members of the group and also gave rise to huge debate about the nature of the transition from feudalism to capitalism. And as well as Dobb, there was Victor Kiernan, John Saville, George Rudé, Rodney Hilton, A L Morton, Dorothy Thompson and Raphael Samuel.

The members of the Historians' Group were Marxists who sought to relate theory to practice, to relate an understanding of

145

the past to both the present and the future. For them the 16th and 17th centuries, medieval and agrarian history, were not simply academic questions but were intimately connected with an understanding of the present. Their overall achievements are magnificent in many ways, the breadth and quality of their historical work is remarkable, their writing a delight. Their books are a lasting education for future generations of socialists. But there are also political lessons to be drawn by socialists today about the weaknesses of the group's theoretical and political analysis, and how those weaknesses informed both their practice as Marxists and their writing of history. But before examining these weaknesses, it is worth looking a little at the workings of the group itself and the historical period that forged its members.

Ten key years

The members of the group were part of a generation shaped by the experience of the 1930s and the Second World War. Thompson, for example, joined the CP in 1942 while studying history at Cambridge University. He was radicalised by the Depression of the 1930s and the rise of the Nazis. He thought the most important thing was to stop Hitler, saying, 'We must place our bodies between fascism and our freedom.' The experience of fighting in Italy during the Second World War and the general radicalisation at the end of the war had a lasting impact on him. He wrote of how at the end of war:

> In liberated Italy I would mooch around the town, find the blacksmith's shop, 'the oxen lifted on a hoist to be shoed' notice the PCI posters, introduce myself as a comrade, and in a trice I would be seated on a bench, incongruous in my British officer's uniform, sampling the blacksmith's wine. It was the same with my comrades in India, Iraq, Egypt... A million informal transactions and discourses were going on in those days, which historians will never recover and which the hard-nosed party organisers knew nothing about.[1]

This was a theme Thompson was to come back to time and again in his writings.

Eric Hobsbawm was influenced similarly by this period. Hobsbawm was born in Egypt, his mother was Austrian, his father the son of a Russian Jewish immigrant. He grew up in

Vienna and Berlin but his family fled Berlin in 1933 when Hitler came to power. He describes in one of his essays why he became a revolutionary socialist:

> What could young Jewish intellectuals have become under such circumstances? Not liberals of any kind, since the world of liberalism (which included social democracy) was precisely what had collapsed. As Jews we were precluded by definition from supporting parties based on confessional allegiance, or on a nationalism which excluded Jews, and in both cases on anti-semitism. We became either Communists or some equivalent form of revolutionary Marxists, or if we chose our own version of blood and soil nationalism, Zionists. There was virtually no other choice. We did not make a commitment against bourgeois society and capitalism, since it patently seemed to be on its last legs. We simple chose a future rather than no future, which meant revolution. But it meant revolution not in a negative but in a positive sense: a new world rather than no world.[2]

Although the group formally still exists today, the most important years of the group were its first ten, 1946 to 1956, the decade immediately following the end of the Second World War. The group grew out of a conference held to discuss the second edition of A L Morton's book *A Peoples' History of England,* which had first been published in 1938. Informal discussions had also led to the publication of Hill's 1940 essay *The English Revolution*, but a formal group was not established until after the war. The group had a chairman, a secretary and a committee, it had subs and organised pool-fares for meetings.

The group was also organised into different 'period' sections: ancient, medieval, the 16th and 17th centuries, the 19th century. It met in London mainly, though there were some activities in localities and local groups were set up. It had a bulletin, *Our History*, and in 1952 its members were key players in the launch of *Past and Present* which became a leading historical journal, a forum for Marxists and non-Marxists alike.

Eric Hobsbawm provides an atmospheric description of the working of the group. In an essay on the group he describes who was involved and goes on:

> These were the people who would make their way, normally at weekends, through what memory recalls mainly as the dank, cold

and slightly foggy morning streets of Clerkenwell to Marx House or to the upper room of the Garibaldi Restaurant, Laystall Street, armed with cyclostyled agendas, sheets of 'theses' or summary arguments, for the debates of the moment. Saffron Hill, Farringdon Road and Clerkenwell Green in the first ten post-war years were not a sybaritic or even a welcoming environment. Physical austerity, intellectual excitement, political passion and friendship are probably what the survivors of those years remember best—but also a sense of equality.[3]

Records from 1951 show that the group set themselves three aims: the extension of 'knowledge and understanding of history through the party and the labour movement as a weapon in the struggle for socialism'; the 'development of independent work among historians and history teachers'; the 'provision of historical material needed by the party'.[4]

This makes clear the way the group sought to tie together Marxist theory with practice to change society. But there were a number of very important weaknesses with the group from the very start. They were all, whether they liked it or not, apologists for Stalinism. Hobsbawm wrote, 'We felt that Marxism implied membership of the party. To criticise Marxism was to criticise the party, and the other way round'.[5] Thompson was to cut out chunks of his book about William Morris for its second edition because of its Stalinist formulations.

Theoretically this meant the group's members were committed to a belief in slow, evolutionary progress; the inevitable development of the forces of production that would eventually lead to the triumph of socialism—though this was not always evident from their history writing. It also led to the group's members making a tacit agreement with the party leadership that they would not touch the history of the British labour movement in the 20th century. They discussed doing this, they knew that it was a major and important task, but they also knew that it meant confronting the role of the CP since its formation in 1920, 'which, as we all knew', says Hobsbawm 'raised some notoriously tricky problems'.[6]

The question of Russia too was largely ignored by the members of the group, except for one early work by Hill. One later study of *Our History* found that between 1956 and 1992 there is not a single article dealing with any aspect of Soviet history.[7] Furthermore, the group's politics cut them off from what is probably the greatest work of Marxist history, Trotsky's *History of the Russian Revolution,* though they were aware of, and read, C L R James' *Black Jacobins*, 'in spite of the author's known Trotskyism'.[8]

The notion of a specialist 'history group' was also quite a contradictory one. It should be a strange notion to Marxists who must all be economists, historians, sociologists and political analysts because Marxism fuses all elements together for a total picture of society. But there is no doubt the members saw the group's specialisation as an advantage. Hill later recalled that:

> The best academic historical training I ever got was from the Historians' Group of the CP where we discussed...science and the revolution, literature and the revolution and so on. That gave me the sort of education that all historians ought to have, it showed me that all individual aspects of history are linked.[9]

The group's first ten years were brought to an abrupt end by the events of 1956. Khrushchev's 'secret' speech followed by the Soviet invasion of Hungary produced an explosion inside the British CP. Many members of the Historians' Group were central to the revolt. Thompson and Saville were suspended from the party for producing the *Reasoner*, a photocopied discussion document, and then resigned. Thompson wrote, 'The Polish and Hungarian people have written their critiques of Stalinism upon their streets and squares. In doing so they have brought back honour to the international Communist movement.' The *Reasoner* became the *New Reasoner* and then merged to form *New Left Review*. Christopher Hill left the party in 1957 after taking part in the party's Commission on Inner Party Democracy. Many other leading historians left the party and the history group was decimated in the process.

Following the events of 1956 the members and ex-members of the group were to go in different directions. But despite the organisational and political break from the party made by many of the CP historians, there is a remarkable degree of continuity in their work that suggests that their break with Stalinism was only partial and left them with a number of theoretical and political weaknesses. There are a number of themes in the historians' work that highlight these weaknesses. This essay will discuss these themes with reference to three of the leading figures of the group, Thompson and Hill, who left the party, and Eric Hobsbawm, who stayed.

149

The role of economic and subjective factors in history

This weakness is present in much of the writing of the history group's members but it is most clear in the work of Edward Thompson, without doubt a brilliant historian and one of the most original members of the group. His reaction against Stalinism led him to seek to rethink Marxism. He sought, as he put it, to restore to Marxism 'the ingredient of humanity'. This lead him to look again at the relationship between economic and subjective factors in history and the use of Marx's metaphor of base and superstructure.

The weaknesses of Thompson's 'rethinking' of Marxism are seen in his most famous book, *The Making of the English Working Class* (1963). This book is a masterpiece in many ways. It is an understandable attempt to reject the crude materialism of Stalinism by emphasising the role played by human agency in shaping history. As a result of this emphasis the book is a remarkably inspiring and positive work. Thompson writes, 'The working class did not rise like the sun at an appointed time, it was present in its own making.' And he famously states his aim is to 'rescue the poor stockinger, the Luddite cropper, the "obsolete" hand-loom weaver, the "utopian" artisan, and even the deluded follower of Joanna Southcott from the enormous condescension of posterity'.[10]

But in his efforts to reject mechanical materialism, Thompson throws the baby out with the bath water. In the preface to the book he offers his celebrated definition of class:

> By class I understand a historical phenomenon… I do not see class as a structure, nor even as a 'category', but as something which in fact happens (and can be shown to have happened) in human relationships… Class is defined by men as they live their own history, and, in the end, this is its only definition… I am convinced that we cannot understand class unless we see it as a social and cultural formation arising from processes which can only be studied as they work themselves out over a considerable historical period.[11]

This is a seriously mistaken approach to class. Classes are structures, they are not just groups of people united by shared views. For Marxists, classes are defined by material interests, by whether a group owns and controls the means of production or whether they do not, and classes stand in relation to one another irrespective of the views of either the rulers or the ruled.

By placing such a subjective emphasis on class, Thompson's definition begs serious questions. Does the working class cease to be a class in periods of low levels of class consciousness? Are there objective processes that shape the patterns of working class struggle? Why can ruling class ideas gain a grip at times, and not at other times? Moreover, the working class is constantly reshaped by changes in capitalism. New groups are thrown up and it may take a period of struggle to forge class consciousness amongst them, but their objective material interests remain the same, and it is those objective material interests that provide the basis for unity in struggle that forges class consciousness.

This is how Marx describes the birth of working class and its consciousness:

> Economic conditions had first transformed the mass of the people of the country into workers. The domination of capital has created for this mass a common situation, common interests. This mass is thus already a class against capital, but not yet for itself. In the struggle...this mass becomes united, and constitutes itself as a class for itself. The interests it defends become class interests.[12]

Struggle for Marx *changes* the working class, struggle for Thompson *creates* the working class.

Thompson's reaction against Stalinism and his theoretical approach to class is reflected in the main body of *The Making of the English Working Class*. The advent of industrial capitalism is the backcloth of the book, not the object of analysis in its own right. This is a serious weakness because to understand the patterns of working class struggle it is necessary to understand how industry develops historically; the way that its geographical spread is uneven. Why do industries vary from region to region? What effect does this have on local struggles? Cotton, iron and coal were all crucial to the first phase of industrialisation in Britain yet these workers barely get a mention in Thompson's book. This is not special pleading: objectively their development was crucial for the development of capitalism and for the British working class as a whole.

The process of capital accumulation needs to be integrated into   151 any historical analysis in order to understand how capitalism constantly shapes and reshapes the working class. To have a total picture of society it is necessary to examine both the objective and the subjective factors that are at play in any particular period. To ignore the underlying economic contradictions in a society is to weaken the power of historical materialism, not develop it. Economic pressures shape the actions of the ruling class, the behaviour of the state and workers' struggles. This combination of objective and subjective factors is neatly summarised by Marx in a famous passage from the *Eighteenth Brumaire of Napoleon Bonaparte*:

> Men make their own history, but they do not make it just as they please; they do not make it under circumstances chosen by themselves, but under circumstances directly encountered, given and transmitted from the past.[13]

Perry Anderson, in *Arguments within English Marxism*, also suggests that the very title of Thompson's book begs a question: was the process finished in 1832?[14]

Thompson, however, is an immensely contradictory writer. There is, of course, economic analysis within *The Making of the English Working Class*. At times he writes of underlying economic developments and points to the objective limits to human actions. But what is true is that Thompson is generally weak at integrating economic and subjective factors to forge a total picture—precisely what Marxism needs to be able to do.

Connected to Thompson's definition of class is his view of the base and superstructure metaphor which Marx used to make a distinction between the economic base of society and the 'corresponding' set of legal and social institutions to which it gives rise. Thompson explicitly rejects this metaphor, arguing that this reduces 'human consciousness to a form of erratic, involuntary response to steel mills and brickyards, which are in a spontaneous process of looming and becoming'.

But Thompson's presentation of base and superstructure is nothing but a crude parody of Marx's original meaning. Marx argues that the level of development of the productive forces and corresponding social relations of production shape all the institutions of society. For example, it is not possible under feudalism, given the level of development of the productive forces, to have the institutions and legal system of modern capitalism.

152

Thompson's rejection of base and superstructure produces some enormous contradictions in his writing, and throws him back on some familiar liberal arguments. In *Whigs and Hunters* (1975) Thompson provides a fascinating analysis of the Black Act of 1723 that created 50 new capital offences aimed at 'wicked and evil-disposed men going armed in disguise' pillaging the royal forests of deer and conducting a running battle against forest officers. With their 'faces blacked' they stole deer, poached hares or fish, cut down trees and set fire to houses or barns in forests.

The Black Act created new offences for malicious shooting, the maiming of cattle. These were made capital offences if the person was armed or disguised or if the offences were committed within the king's forests. The book traces why the act was passed, how it was applied and its effects on people. The act was a clear defence of private property. Thompson points to how it was used often in the context of resistance to enclosures, when people would shoot into houses or maim cattle to get back at those evicting them from their land. It was repealed 100 years later, after prolonged resistance.

Whigs and Hunters, however, also includes a section on 'the rule of law' in which Thompson criticises right wing and Whig views that present the 18th century as an era of peace and stability but which also attacks the Marxist notion that the law is part of the superstructure, and he rejects the notion that law serves the interests of the ruling class. He says he partially accepts a Marxist framework, and admits that his book at times shows exactly that view of the law, but insists also that the law must be seen in terms of its own logic, rules and procedures. Thompson writes:

> If we suppose that law is no more than a mystifying and pompous way in which class power is registered and executed, then we need not waste our labour in studying its history and its forms. One act would be much the same as another, and all, from the standpoint of the ruled, would be Black. It is because law matters that we have bothered with this study at all.[15]

And in his efforts to reject a mechanical Marxist interpretation of base and superstructure he falls back on the very liberal view he attacks, saying, 'This study has focused on a bad law, drawn by bad legislators, and enlarged by the interpretations of bad judges...this study does not prove that all law is bad'.[16]

153

This is not just a historical question: Thompson was also writing about contemporary questions. In the 1970s he became increasingly concerned about the growth of the 'secret state' and invasions of civil liberties. He returned to praise the rule of law in a *New Society* article, describing it as 'unqualified human good' and 'a cultural achievement of universal significance' without any hint of qualification. Not only is this view mistaken, it is as simplistic as the Stalinist view he attacks.[17]

Thompson's weaknesses are also seen clearly in his critique of the French Marxist philosopher and academic Louis Althusser. Thompson was right to take up the cudgels against Althusser and the dehumanised form of Marxism Althusser spawned in the 1970s and 1980s. But in his essay *The Poverty of Theory*, Thompson lumps Marx and Althusser together. He says both Marx and Althusser have nothing to say about the value systems people construct to make sense of their experience because they see values as just bourgeois morality. Thompson accuses Marx's *Capital* of being little different from the political economy Marx criticised, writing:

> Political economy has terms for use value, for exchange value, for monetary value, and for surplus value but not for normative value. It has no terms for other areas of consciousness.[18]

Hence Thompson, in his efforts to seeks to restore the 'moral dimension' to Marxism that he thinks is lacking, is prepared to dismiss Marx's analysis of the laws of motion of capitalist society and the creation of a working class that is pushed by objective forces to struggle collectively. But without these elements there is the danger that Marxism is reduced to a moral critique of capitalism alone, one that washes out the issue of class.

Populism

Another weakness present in the work of the Historians' Group is the blurring of the division between class and 'the people'. This stems from the politics of the popular front that influenced them all during their formative political years. The theory of the popular front was adopted by Communist parties across the world in the 1930s and 1940s. The CP opposed the Second World War, for example, as an imperialist war until the German invasion of the Soviet Union in 1941. It then flipped over into being an enthusiastic supporter of the war and sought a broad class alliance to defeat Nazism. In the 1940s the CP line became that there are different, national roads to socialism and that socialists should collaborate with 'progressive' and 'patriotic' sections of capital.

The influence of this approach on the group can be seen in a number of ways. Remember the title of Morton's book, *A People's History of England*. Similarly, the early activities of the group included a conference in Nottingham in 1952 on 'The History of the British People's Opposition to War'. Rodney Hilton made a passionate speech to the group in 1951 in which he attacked the 'history from above' of the ruling class that leaves out the masses and concluded that the problem was 'to give back to the British people its true history' and that 'it was the responsibility of Communists almost alone at first to lead the fight for true British history'.[19]

This political approach is also present in Christopher Hill's 1958 essay 'The Norman Yoke', in which he shows how English radicals from the 17th century well into the 19th century tended to see the ruling class as an alien group as a result of the Norman Conquest. This idea is then used to justify a populist alliance of all classes against foreign rule.[20]

The politics of the popular front are also present in the work of Eric Hobsbawm. In many respects Hobsbawm remains a very orthodox Marxist. His history contains a great deal of analysis of objective economic process and he criticises the work of the early history group on the grounds that 'we were not, on the whole, very strong on the economic side of economic history'.[21] The framework for *The Age of Revolution* (1962) is very strong. He talks of the dual revolution, the Industrial Revolution in Britain and the revolution in France as the two key events in shaping the modern world. Similarly *The Age of Empire* (1987), which covers the period between 1875 and 1914, is framed within the theory of imperialism as developed by Lenin and Bukharin, the changes in liberal capitalist economies in the mid-19th century that produce a more broadly based world economy, no longer dominated by Britain. He talks of the accelerating concentration and centralisation of capital and the growing convergence of politics and economics as the basis of the partition of the globe into colonial empires.

But a big weakness present in *The Age of Empire*, however, is   155

Hobsbawm's tendency to conflate the labour movement with the working class. He presents the working 'classes' as fragmented, divided by skill, occupation, gender, language, religion and nationality. There is little sense of the working class being defined by its relationship to the means of production which provides the objective basis for unity in struggle. Instead Hobsbawm says a disembodied 'labour movement' is necessary to unite workers. He writes, 'It was through the movement that the plural "working classes" were fused into a singular "working class" '.[22]

This leads on to a rather dubious analysis of nationalism in which Hobsbawm writes, 'The effective framework of their class consciousness was, except at brief moments of revolution, the state and the politically defined nation'.[23] So the working class acquires its identity from a movement oriented on winning control of the existing nation state. When these parties become electorally unpopular, Hobsbawm regards it as threatening the working class itself—precisely the analysis offered by Hobsbawm from the late 1970s onwards.

Hobsbawm became a leading figure in providing an intellectual justification of the political shift to the right that was made by large sections of the British left in the 1980s. He argued that the working class movement was on the retreat; its social base eroded by economic changes, its political advance halted. He was an active instigator of the Eurocommunist wing of the CP's pursuit of what it called realignment on the left, of pursuing a broad cross-class alliance against Thatcherism. He went as far as to argue in the pages of *Marxism Today* for tactical voting.

Nationalism

Another lasting continuity in the work of the CP historians is revealed in their treatment of nationalism. They do not break from the framework established by CPs in the early 1950s that was essentially a continuation of their policy during the war— that of national roads to socialism and the framework of the nation not the revolutionary internationalism of the classical Marxist tradition.

This is evident in Hobsbawm's analysis of the labour movement, and it is also clear in the writing of Edward Thompson. For example when approaching the question of the Common Market in the 1970s, Thompson describes 1975 as a 'time of unparalleled socialist opportunity' in Britain if the country did not enter the Common Market.

> One can glimpse, as an outside chance, the possibility that we could effect here a peaceful transition—for the first time in the world—to a democratic socialist society... The lines of British culture still run vigorously towards the point of change where our traditions and organisations cease to be defensive and become affirmative forces: the country becomes our own.[24]

In many ways this sums up the lasting influence of the CP on Thompson's politics: it is the reformist, cross-class, nationalist politics of the popular front. This tendency to approach history in largely English, national terms is present elsewhere in Thompson's work. In his *Open Letter to Leszek Kolakowski* (1973) he talks about 'our' rate of growth compared to Europe's and about whether 'English apples can stand up to French competition'.[25] In the same essay Thompson also puts up a spirited defence of the 'English' intellectual idiom:

> Take Marx and Vico and a few European novelists away, and my most intimate pantheon would be a provincial tea party: a gathering of the English, the Anglo-Irish. Talk of free will and determinism, and I think first of Milton. Talk of man's inhumanity, I think of Swift. Talk of morality and revolution, and my mind is off with Wordsworth's 'Solitary'. Talk of the problems of self activity and creative labour in socialist society, and I am in an instant back with William Morris.[26]

Pessimism

A final weakness is a tendency to pessimism. This is revealed clearly in Hill's work on the 17th century. In some ways of all the group's members Hill emerges with the strongest record, although this must partly be because he ventures little outside the 17th century. His writings on the 17th century are peppered with references to more contemporary issues. There are frequent sideswipes at Thatcherism, for example, but these attacks are never integrated into anything more substantial.

Hill also retreats from the defence of a total view of the English Revolution that is contained in *The English Revolution* and *Century of Revolution*. Both these books integrate the class struggle in its economic context. Later he moves to detailed accounts of partial and often cultural aspects of the revolution from the *World Turned Upside Down* (1972) onwards. This is a brilliant book, but also one that begs many questions about what were the economic and social limits to change being fought for by the Levellers and the other radical groups. As a result there is a growing separation between Hill's overall theoretical defence of a Marxist interpretation of the English Revolution, his commitment to total history and his actual history writing. The two are often not integrated and Hill says he explicitly rejected using Marxist terminology very early on.[27]

There is also a political pessimism that affects Hill's work. This comes across very clearly in the *Experience of Defeat* (1984) that continues some of the themes begun in *The World Turned Upside Down*. In *The World Turned Upside Down* Hill looked at the hopes of the radical sects produced by the English Revolution—the Ranters, the Seekers, the Fifth Monarchists, the Muggletonians. He shows how the overthrow of the monarchy took the lid off English society and allowed social and religious experimentation to flourish briefly. The Diggers especially sought a social revolution where heaven would be brought down to earth and the land owned in common. The Radicals' hopes were dashed by Cromwell's Protectorate and then by the restoration of the monarchy in 1660. This experience of defeat is then examined further through the work of Milton.

The Experience of Defeat widens the focus of *The World Turned Upside Down* to consider how all the revolutionaries respond to the collapse of their hopes after Cromwell and his allies, having used the Levellers to help dispose of the king, then turned to crush them and the Diggers in turn. Hill shows how in the 1650s the revolutionaries increasingly come to fear the masses and begin to talk of the necessity of rule by an enlightened minority. Milton argues for an oligarchy, other radicals look to the army as a guarantor of liberty.

Hill goes on to make the fatal mistake of conflating the experience of bourgeois and socialist revolutions. He compares Milton's substitutionism with the Bolsheviks' substitution after the disintegration of the Russian working class. 'Similarly the New Model Army substituted itself for the people of England,' writes Hill. He constantly compares the defeated radicals with Marxists of the 20th century. Milton, for example, is compared with Lenin during the years of reaction after the revolution of 1905. 'In 1644 Milton saw England as a "nation of prophets". Where are the prophets now?' writes Hill in virtually the last line of the book.[28]

These sentiments are not accidental. It seems that Hill no longer believes in the Stalinist view of inevitable progress, his pessimism leads him to identify with the revolution's defeated minorities, the disillusion with Cromwell is comparable to the disillusion with Stalin. But bourgeois revolutions are not comparable with socialist revolutions in this way. Bourgeois revolutions involve, of necessity, class alliances. They are carried out by minorities who need to mobilise broader forces but fear where that mobilisation might lead. Socialist revolutions are, of necessity, revolutions of the majority in society, for the majority of society and cannot rely on the acts of an enlightened minority.

Conclusion

The founding members of the Communist Party Historians' Group are in many ways far better than those who claim to follow them today. Many of the followers of 'history from below', by taking Thompson's preface to *The Making of the English Working Class* as their theoretical framework, exaggerate one of his greatest weaknesses. The Marxist view of history is not just about tiny details and oral histories. History is not simply concerned with what people say or about people's experience. Marxists need to seek a total picture of society, but one that combines an understanding of base and superstructure, of consciousness and determination, in order to understand how 'men make history but not in circumstances of their own choosing'.

The great strength of the Historians' Group was that it linked theory and practice together, albeit in a distorted, Stalinist way. But Stalinism left its mark on the group's writing of history. Those who did break with Stalinism never replaced it with an alternative rounded theoretical tradition—instead their rejection of Stalinism left them theoretically weakened. Socialists today stand in great debt to them but we must also reject their theoretical and practical limitations.

CHAPTER 9

Revolutionary Marxism and academic Marxism

John Rees

Marxism is 'the theory of the conditions of the liberation of the proletariat' in Engels' famous formulation.[1] And, as such, it relies on close contact with the development of the class struggle not only for its ultimate purpose but also for its vitality and relevance as a theory. Yet much of what has claimed the mantle of Marxism in the 20th century, particularly during its second half, has been developed within the academic institutions of capitalist society, institutions which often pride themselves on their social neutrality, on their lack of contact with social forces of any description. This was not always the way, especially for those thinkers who pioneered the world view of the modern ruling class.

There is a very noticeable rupture in the development of the ideology of the bourgeoisie in the period between the great French Revolution of 1789 and the aftermath of the Europe wide revolutions of 1848. This was a watershed. Before it the bourgeoisie were still antagonistic toward the old semi-feudal order but, after it, they became more frightened of the rising working class than they were of the old order. This important change had ideological ramifications that can be traced across the work of philosophers, economists and historians.

In the heroic period of the bourgeoisie's development, beginning with the English and Scottish philosophers of the 17th century, notably Thomas Hobbes, John Locke, David Hume, and culminating in the great Enlightenment tradition of the French Encylopaedists in the 18th century—Diderot, Voltaire, Rousseau—

161

philosophers tended to champion the cause of scientific reason in the face of superstition and mysticism. The most outstanding inheritors of this philosophical estate, the German philosophers Immanuel Kant and G W F Hegel, were to develop a more critical tone, both continuing the belief in the power of rational thought and also debating its limitations. But, after the decline of the Hegelian school in all its variants by the late 1840s, no similar grand bourgeois theory ever attempted such an all embracing explanation of the relationship between philosophy and society. Within a generation of 1848 the bourgeoisie were less in need of the sharp scalpel of philosophical thought in order to cut away at the ideological tissue of the old order. They either were in power, in France, Britain and the United States, or would soon be so by coming to an accommodation with the older aristocratic elements of the ruling class, often leading to the latter's longer term eclipse, as in Germany, Italy and even Japan.

The same ebb tide can be seen running through economic analysis. Marx watched it first hand and drew a distinction between the classical economists such as Adam Smith and David Ricardo, whose work genuinely began to uncover the workings of the capitalist economy, and the later 'vulgar' economists in which ideology had replaced analysis even to the extent of obscuring some of the scientific advances of their predecessors' work. Ricardo's labour theory of value, for instance, was only developed and defended by Marx and Engels. It was largely abandoned by the new establishment economists. The same process has been observed in the development of modern sociology:

> It is clear why a connection exists between the development of modern sociology and conservative political thought. It is the product of a crisis in which the forms of both theoretical and practical thought developed by the bourgeoisie in its revolutionary period were being fundamentally rejected by the intellectual representatives of the same class, just as they were being critically absorbed into the new theory of those whose standpoint was that of the proletariat. The 'rational kernel' of political economy, like that of classical philosophy, became anathema to bourgeois thought just as it was an inspiration to Marx. Hegel had written that in his time 'revolution was lodged and expressed as if in the very form of thought'. Now it was counter-revolution which was expressed in the form of thought of sociology.[2]

The study of history was by no means immune from this process. There had been a long tradition of gentleman-amateur scholars writing history in England—how could it be otherwise before the development of an extensive university system free of clerical control. These were historians who were often political actors in their own right. John Milton (1608-74) is best known for *Paradise Lost*, itself an intensely political commentary on the events of the English Revolution of the 1640s. He is less well known for his *History of Britain* and for his role as Secretary for Foreign Tongues in Cromwell's republic. From the same era, Milton's foe, the royalist Edward Hyde (1609-74), later Earl of Clarendon, was both adviser to Charles I and author of *The History of the Great Rebellion*. In a later generation Edward Gibbon (1737-94), was an MP when he wrote *Decline and Fall of the Roman Empire*, as was Thomas Macaulay (1800-59) when he wrote his *History of England*. The separation of history and political activity, later the hallmark of 'serious' academic work, was unknown to some of the greatest thinkers of this crucial era in the development of modern society.

The more capitalist society developed and prospered, the more the educational institutions which it nurtured (and which nurtured it) became detached from immediate involvement in political affairs. Specialisation developed as quickly in the academy as it did in the factory. According to Lawrence Stone:

> Between 1870 and 1930, history developed into an independent professional discipline in its own right. Separate history departments were created in the universities, PhD programs for the training and accreditation of future professionals were instituted, professional associations were formed. Meanwhile, the prime subject matter of history, under the influence of the bourgeois liberal nationalism of the age, was defined as the administrative and constitutional evolution of the nation state and the diplomatic and military relationships between those states. National record offices were set up, and the basic documents relating to these issues were…made available to scholars…[3]

As this professionalisation gathered pace that part of the older tradition which valued depicting society as a whole, and which tried at worst to describe and at best to explain large scale changes in society suffered correspondingly. But it did not disappear. Rather academic history has tended to reproduce two distinct responses to growing institutionalisation. On the one hand there have been no shortage of historians who have followed the empiricist path of assuming that the mere accumulation of facts without any acknowledged theoretical framework is the very stuff of historical enquiry. Often but not always such an approach is accompanied by a drastic narrowing of focus, encouraged by the requirement that 'original research' is necessary to gain a doctorate. The result is that we know more and more about less and less—perhaps the most infinitesimal details of a feudal serf's diet, but not the relations of land ownership which determined that diet. Lawrence Stone observes:

> These...scholars were content to elaborate on the problems and techniques established by 1900 and describe in ever more minute detail discrete events, mainly political or administrative, without showing much desire to relate these events to anything else or render them meaningful to more than a handful of fellow workers in that very specialised vineyard.[4]

A similar complaint was made by the overwhelming majority, some 74 percent, of the 1,000 respondents to the 1994 survey by the Organization of American Historians who agreed that 'the academic reward system encourages historians to write for academic audiences and discourages historians from reaching multiple audiences'. Some respondents appended their own elaboration of the point. One insisted that academic historians were afraid of 'writing clear, dramatic, interesting narrative, which may be interpreted by colleagues as unsophisticated or lacking theoretical understanding' while another complained of 'elite monographs...not accessible to educated lay persons' which are 'written by incredibly boring academics. No one reads it. Who can blame them?'[5]

Such elitism and specialisation are not, however, accidental. Ultimately, they have their root in the class divisions of capitalist society which necessarily engender divisions between intellectual life and the rest of society, just as surely as the monks who illuminated manuscripts in a medieval monastery were separated from the lives of the peasants around them. But, once such separations become institutionalised in the modern university, they develop a momentum of their own:

> Disciplinary and professional mechanisms within each of the

'social sciences' limit the development of thought and maintain a degree of fragmentation which is quite extreme… The academic organisation of social knowledge requires, in order to keep the work of individual researchers within established forms and processes, the existence of a large number of discrete disciplines. The re-division of the social sciences into more and more narrow fields, which continues apace, admirably serves the purpose of the academic structure of social knowledge. The more narrow the definition of the field, the more specific the technical forms of research can be, the more rigid and formal the substantive standards which operate. In addition [this] satisfies the specific financial and prestige requirements of rising intellectual groups…[6]

In reaction, a minority of historians have kept to the goal of trying to capture something of the grand sweep of historical change, but often at the expense of any concrete knowledge. Windy generalisation replaced close, articulated argument. These writers, who were 'reacting somewhat extravagantly to the ever-narrower empiricism of their colleagues, went to the other extreme and became macrotheorists, either visionaries with global models of evolution, like Spengler or Toynbee, or men working at a lower level of theoretical generalisation'.[7] One obvious modern example of this kind of approach is Francis Fukuyama's pseudo-Hegelian musings on the 'end of history'. More seriously, Paul Kennedy's otherwise useful *The Rise and Fall of Great Powers* was marred by its overly simplistic framework of 'imperial overreach' whereby all major powers grow, fail to sustain their ambitious military empires and decline. By the time Kennedy's next book, *Preparing for the Twenty-First Century*, was written an even more simplistic Malthusianism had all but entirely vitiated any historical insight.[8] But the trend long predates this outbreak. Sociological 'system builders' from Marx and Engels' old foe, the German academic Eugen Dühring, to the contemporary school of historical sociologists, like Anthony Giddens, also exemplify this trend.[9]

These then are the hallmarks of history writing in the dominant educational institutions of capitalist society: specialisation breeds empiricism, which in turn produces, as a counteraction, an idealism dependent on simplistic generalisation and increasingly devoid of any connection with a concrete analysis. The hierarchical and self validating structure of academic life makes these ideological approaches particularly impervious to challenge by non-academics. And the increasing commodification of academic life, the 'publish or be sacked' ethos which grew with the market oriented counter-revolution of the 1980s, has made it all the more difficult for academics themselves to challenge the bias of the institutions in which they work.

Challenges to the limits of academia

The increasingly constricted limits of academia have, of course, regularly been challenged especially by those bringing wider experience to bear on the cloistered halls of educational institutions. From Milton's oration 'Against Scholastic Philosophy' to the gathered colleges of Cambridge, when he told them of their 'ignorance and absurd childishness when faced with a new situation outside their usual idiotic occupation' the result of which was to 'make you a more finished fool and a clever contriver of conceits, and to endow you with a more expert ignorance', there have stretched a long line of revolts, individual and collective, against the claustrophobia of the educational system.[10]

As the educational system has become more adapted to the demands of late capitalist development, these revolts have been of two interlinked types. As the numbers admitted to the system have increased, particularly in the industrialised world in the last 50 years, the elite nature of higher education has been modified. Although still overwhelmingly the preserve of the middle classes, with the addition of a small percentage of children from working class backgrounds, it is no longer true that the universities are simply the training schools of the ruling class. The complexity of modern capitalism requires that a somewhat higher level of knowledge is more widely dispersed among the population.

This transformation has also altered the likely political allegiance of the students. It is difficult to imagine contemporary students organised into drinking clubs with fascist sympathies, as in pre-war Germany, or to scab on a general strike, as they were in Britain in 1926. Indeed, students have formed an important component of such widely varied social protest movements as the anti Vietnam War protests, CND, the National Abortion Campaign, the Anti Nazi League, the Anti-Apartheid Movement and many others, as well as mounting frequent protests over their own conditions, academic and material.

But this is only part of the story. There have also been related developments concerning the content of what is taught in colleges, challenges to the establishment view of what defines relevant or acceptable knowledge. In the historical sciences one of the most important of these changes in the last 100 years has been the rise of 'the new history', as it was first known, beginning in the 1930s and gathering force during the post-war period until the 1970s. Social history, as it became known, owed in all its forms a great debt to the Marxist tradition. The figures who emerged out of the British Communist Party's Historians' Group remain its best known exponents. Their considerable achievements are evaluated elsewhere in this volume. What is important as far as the argument of this chapter is concerned are the following considerations.

Firstly, this challenge was mounted to the then orthodoxy of the historical profession by people who were political activists as well as historians. The impetus for the revolution that they accomplished in their profession came from a movement and a political organisation outside it. The sustaining element for their critique of the established orthodoxy came, later, from the growth of higher education and then from the student and working class revolts of the 1960s and 1970s.

Secondly, as this sustaining element began to fall away in the late 1970s it has become increasingly obvious that the gains originally made have either been reversed or have been accommodated to a new orthodoxy. The reverses have been partial, but real. The various revisionisms—of French, English and Russian revolutionary history, for instance—have in part made their mark by returning to a form of political history long outdated even in school textbooks, focusing on the psychology of great leaders, the machinations of their coteries and the genealogy of the political institutions which they inhabit.[11]

But perhaps the more interesting development has been the degree to which the challenge of 'history from below' has become sanitised by partial incorporation into the syllabus structure of modern history teaching. Lawrence Stone, himself one of the beneficiaries of this process, writes that 'the change from 1965 to 1975 is startling':

> Today a casual glance at the program [of the American Historical Association annual convention] gives the impression that hardly any work is in progress in America which is not concerned with

167

the subject matter of the oppressed and inarticulate—slaves, the poor, or women—with problems such as social structure and mobility, the family and sex, crime and deviance, popular culture and witchcraft, and which is not using social science theories…[12]

Even in the way in which Stone formulates the issue we can trace a marked change from the original concerns of the Marxist pioneers of social history. They were certainly concerned to widen the ambit of study, to write the history of those 'hidden from history' in Sheila Rowbotham's phrase. But they did not think that everything that had been previously excluded was equally worthy of rediscovery, or of equal interest were it to be rediscovered. They might have balked at one consequence of their achievements when they saw in a recent edition of *Past and Present*, once the flagship of the new history, the beginning of an article on 'The Decline of Falconry in Early Modern England':

Field sports are a neglected subject even in the new social history. This is surprising because…gentlemen spent more time in the field than in church or at the theatre. Hunting rituals…illuminate…the rituals and mores of pre-industrial society.[13]

Whatever else can be said of the article which follows, it does not 'illuminate the mores of pre-industrial society' in the way that perhaps a study of an institution as central to that society as the church might have done. The difficulty is that, in the name of social history, horizons are narrowing once again; it can again be said that many historians choose to tell us more and more about less and less. 'It certainly looks', to Stone at least, 'as if the triumph of the "new historians" has brought into being signs of a new illusion of value-free science, a new dogmatism, and a new scholasticism that threaten to become as stifling and sterile as those which first came under attack 40 years ago'.[14]

The argument is not that there is no point in struggling to establish a historical tradition which seeks to understand the experience of the exploited and the oppressed—there obviously is. Neither is it to assert that there is nothing to choose between competing right wing and left wing currents in academia. Again, there clearly is. The argument is that such opportunities to represent the history of the exploited and oppressed do not rest primarily on the turn of events in academia itself. Such opportunities arise from developments among the struggles of the oppressed and exploited themselves, from their own political and social organisations. Such academic currents as emerge as a consequence of these struggles are not self sustaining. If the struggles themselves subside then their theoretical reflection withers, perhaps not immediately or completely but nevertheless decisively, until it is once again acceptable to the prevailing power structure in academia and society at large.

Rosa Luxemburg may have been exaggerating for polemical purpose when she said that 'German social scientists always function as an extension of the police', but she was right to assume that academic institutions as a whole are as impervious to fundamental change as the security apparatus of the state. Educational institutions, run by and funded by the capitalist state can be made to bend by the force of social struggles. They can be forced by the impact of those same struggles to tolerate, for greater or longer periods, currents of theoretical opposition. But they cannot as a whole become permanently detached in any fundamental way from the interests of the ruling class. They cannot become, therefore, a base of opposition to the existing system for those who wish to change the system.

The social basis of the classical Marxist tradition

The social institution on which academic Marxism rests is the educational apparatus of capitalist society. The social basis of revolutionary Marxism is working class struggle. This, however, does not reflect itself in a direct and unmediated way. Clearly, most workers, most of the time do not subscribe to Marxist ideas. Marxism is not a direct reflection of the current consciousness of this or that particular group of workers, but a theory of society constructed from the international and historical experience of the working class. This does not mean, however, that Marxist ideas have no correspondence to reality. They can be verified in a number of different ways. Like any scientific theory, they can be found more or less adequate as an analysis of objective development. If one particular theory, for instance, finds the economies of the South East Asian 'Tiger' capitalisms to be crisis free while other, Marxist, accounts insist that they are not, then these propositions can be evaluated over the appropriate time scale.

Secondly, the fact that most workers do not share Marxist

ideas most of the time, does not preclude a minority of workers from so doing. Marxism can also be evaluated by its success in guiding the actions of this minority, including, crucially, its relations with the majority of non-Marxist workers. And, of course, the ultimate success of Marxism as a theory depends on its ability to successfully create and fuse with a revolutionary movement which does involve the majority of workers in a self conscious movement for their own liberation. Such commitment to action, even in the pre-revolutionary phases of working class struggle, enables Marxist theoreticians to integrate the theoretical work of understanding the world with the practical work of changing it.

This fact was clearly understood by the generations of revolutionaries who form the core of the classical Marxist tradition. Marx and Engels famously wrote *The Communist Manifesto* at the request of the leaders of the Communist League of which they were active members. Later they both laboured to organise the International Workingmen's Association, the first ever international body of trade unionist and socialist militants. Engels went on to become the intellectual guide of the Second International which grouped together the rapidly expanding socialist parties of Europe. For subsequent generations, for Lenin, Trotsky, Luxemburg, Lukács and Gramsci, it was equally axiomatic that the development of Marxist theory and the building of political organisation were necessarily inseparable.

This automatic association of theory and practice, particularly the practice of party building, was broken by the onset of the twin tragedies of fascism and Stalinism. In the first instance this destruction took a brutal and literal form: many of the key figures who embodied the unity of theory and practice were liquidated in the concentration camps of the Nazis and the gulags of Stalinism. Those not physically exterminated, like Trotsky, or imprisoned, like Gramsci, capitulated, like Lukács in the late 1920s, and only enjoyed a sporadic and unsatisfactory relationship to political activity thereafter.

Others found safe refuge in academia. And here, for the first time, a generation of theorists claiming some relationship to the Marxist tradition developed in not-so-splendid isolation from any contact with even a militant minority of the working class movement. As Perry Anderson has observed:

The first and most fundamental of its characteristics has been the structural divorce of this Marxism from political practice. The organic unity of theory and practice realised in the classical generation of Marxists before the First World War, who performed an inseparably politico-intellectual function within their respective parties in Eastern and Central Europe, was to be increasingly severed in the half-century from 1918-1968, in Western Europe.

The chasm between theoreticians and activists did not occur in an instant, 'it was slowly and progressively brought about by massive historical pressures, which only achieved the final breakage of the bond between theory and practice during the 1930s.' Nevertheless, once the rupture had occurred it was so decisive that 'by the epoch after the Second World War...the distance between them was so great that it seemed consubstantial with the tradition' of academic Marxism.[15]

This rupture was in part repaired by the great international uprising which shook the world in 1968 and which rolled on through a series of momentous struggles until the mid-1970s. The Tet Offensive signalled the beginning of the end for US imperialism in Vietnam and the anti-war movement in the US and internationally took confidence from seeing a tiny Third World and guerrilla army humiliate the greatest military machine in human history. The student protests in France detonated the largest general strike in European history. Italy's 'May in slow motion' saw a quadrupling of strike action in a single year. Over 200 US cities burned as rioting followed the assassination of Martin Luther King. The Stalinist monolith cracked during Czechoslovakia's Prague Spring. And, as that revolt fell under Russian tank tracks, tens of thousands left the Western Communist Parties in disgust. Even as late as the mid-1970s the British working class movement dispatched the Tory government, Franco's fascist dictatorship crumbled in Spain, as did the regime of the Greek colonels, and the Portuguese military dictatorship fell to revolution.

Unsurprisingly perhaps, a new unity of theory and practice was discovered, though only in a minority of cases in the same terms as the classical Marxist tradition. Feminism and black liberation did produce a new generation of activists who were, at the same time, theoreticians and writers. So did the movements for national liberation in the Third World. But the ideas which emerged from these currents had a troubled history and found it difficult to sustain their radical charge very long after their explosive point of origin. Cut off from the older tradition of Marxist and socialist analysis they were both practically and theoretically unable to come to terms with the force which still commanded the field as the oldest and most consistent enemy of the system, the organised working class. Consequently, they were less able to resist the ideological and practical pressures encountered as the movements born in 1968 began to decline in late 1970s.

To do so would have required coming to terms with the organisational question. For to combat the still existing, if now more discredited, organisations of the working class, the Communist and social democratic parties, required not a rejection of party organisation, as much of the New Left imagined, but a rediscovery of revolutionary organisation as it had existed before the onset of Stalinism. This, in turn, would have provided the crucible in which a new generation of revolutionary leaders could have worked to renew the theoretical traditions largely dormant from the 1930s to the 1960s.

The conduit which had carried the classical Marxist tradition from before the flood, Trotskyism, had in many of its variants its own distortions. Even in its best incarnations it was simply too small for all but a small stream of the mighty torrent unleashed in 1968 to flow through its channels. But as the torrent subsided the best of the revolutionary tradition has proved more durable than many of the better known ideological formations born of 1968. And it has emerged in the 1990s, as confidence has begun to return to the working class movement internationally, better placed to lay the basis for a rebirth of the classical Marxist tradition than at any time since the 1930s. But to make good that potential requires that today's socialists absorb some of those ideas about the unity of theory and practice which were second nature to the founders of the Marxist tradition.

The roots of revolutionary theory

For revolutionary theory to regain its original force and function requires an overturning of some of the most widely held and cherished assumptions among academic Marxists. Firstly, fruitful developments in revolutionary theory can only emerge in close interrelationship with the struggle of the class whose experience they are meant to generalise. Immersion in the struggle is not to soil oneself with the bias of sectional interests, as so many academics assume, but a method of ensuring that the questions which theory poses, and the answers it attempts to give, are shaped by the experience of the working class and socialist movement, not by the priorities of capitalism's educational hierarchy. To avoid direct involvement in the struggle is not to avoid sectional influence but to replace the influence of the working class movement with that of professional middle class educationalists and their masters.

Secondly, such involvement in the struggle is merely the precondition of effective theoretical work, but it does not automatically ensure that such work will necessarily lead to correct conclusions. To maximise the possibility of success the adoption of a specific method of analysis is necessary. This method has been generalised from the international and historical experience of the working class, including the encounters of previous generations of theorists with the ideological defenders of the establishment, and so it cannot be reduced to the immediate experience of the struggle of the working class at any particular moment. This approach, dialectical materialism, differs in important ways from even the most left wing versions of the social sciences.

Take the notion of totality, for instance, vital to the Marxist method because it insists on the interconnectedness of the social process and provides a guide for relating the various different aspects of the struggle together. Many academics instinctively feel constricted by the compartmentalism of their studies, understanding that economics and politics, art and science, race and class and so on cannot be fully understood within the confines of departmental sectionalism. Yet the revolt against such atomisation of study often gets no further than calls for more 'interdisciplinary studies'. The following was written about the difficulties faced by academic Marxist economists, but the point is valid for other disciplines as well:

> The critic is under immense pressure to compromise intellectually, not to admit the total opposition of assumptions, concepts and methods which must exist between any 'radical' economics and the mainstream. Marx must be transformed into a precursor of Keynes and so forth…The 'marxist economist' is still an economist, a peculiar kind of academic theorist accepting a basic divorce, first of himself from his subject matter, secondly of his subject matter from that which is regarded as the province of sociology,

political theory, etc. Because of its precarious position within the academic sphere, marxist economics faces a very severe demand to define itself in relation to bourgeois economics, and to academic social-scientific concepts in general, rather to working class struggle and to revolutionary thought.[16]

What is ultimately at stake in the conflict between these approaches is not just whether a lecturer from the economics department occasionally gets to speak to philosophy students. The whole nature of the division of labour in capitalist society, ultimately rooted in the division between classes and the division between manual and mental labour which are constitutive of the system, are what underpin the compartmentalism of academic life. To be rid of the debilitating effect of such divisions the theorist needs to place him or herself in a social location where the unity of theory and practice are a precondition of the success of both—that is, in a position where attempting to change the world is a precondition of understanding it, and understanding the world is a precondition of changing it effectively. The class position of the working class is the only such location in modern society.

Such a position cannot be adopted without confronting the issue of revolutionary organisation. The working class struggle is a collective and organised struggle—to be part of it requires that one works collectively and in an organised manner. Such commitment was undertaken by all the major figures in the classical Marxist tradition, but the rise of Stalinism corrupted the circuits which allowed serious theoretical work to emerge as part of organised participation in the working class struggle.

But such circuits will have to be re-established if we are to have an effective socialist organisation or an effective theory. Part of the reason why generations of academic Marxists have failed to contribute as much as they might to the theoretical legacy of the Marxist tradition is because they have misunderstood this notion of partisanship. They thought it only referred to party loyalty, but in actual fact it has a far broader theoretical significance as a barrier to abstraction, determinism and idealism. Lenin summarised the crucial issue:

The objectivist speaks of a necessity of a given historical process; the materialist gives an exact picture of the given socio-economic formation and the antagonistic relation to which it gives rise. When demonstrating the necessity for a given series of facts, the objectivist always runs the risk of becoming an apologist for these facts: the materialist discloses the class contradictions and in so doing defines his standpoint. The objectivist speaks of 'insurmountable historical tendencies'; the materialist speaks of the class which 'directs' the given economic system, giving rise to such and such forms of counteraction by other classes...

Lenin goes on to insist that the uncovering of such contradictions implies a commitment to action:

The materialist would not content himself with stating 'insurmountable historical tendencies', but would point to the existence of certain classes...[which] preclude any solution except by the action of the producers themselves...materialism includes partisanship, so to speak, and enjoins the open adoption of the standpoint of a definite social group in the assessment of events.[17]

A revolutionary organisation is the crucible where the objective historical process and the subjective analysis of how it can be transformed are fused together in an amalgam of analysis and action. Building such an organisation is, therefore, the forum and precondition for development of Marxist theory which can, in Engels' words, serve not as a dogma but as a guide to action.

Notes

CHAPTER 1

1 K Marx and F Engels, *The German Ideology* (C J Arthur (ed), London, 1996), pp42, 47-48.
2 Ibid, p58.
3 P Joyce, 'The End of Social History?', *Social History* XX (1995), p82.
4 See M Haynes, 'Was there a Parliamentary Alternative in Russia in 1917?', *International Socialism* 76, Autumn 1997.
5 R J Evans, *In Defence of History* (London, 1997), p124.

CHAPTER 2

1 Many of the issues raised in this essay are explored in more depth in my book *Theories and Narratives* (Cambridge, 1995). In this essay I have drawn on talks and papers given at Marxism 97; the Nehru Memorial Museum and Library, New Delhi; the Centre for Studies in Social Sciences, Calcutta; the Department of History, Bombay University; and the *International Socialism* History School (Jan 1998). I am grateful to all concerned with these events for their help and comments.
2 G M Trevelyan, *English Social History* (London, 1942), p vii.
3 See S Ashman, 'The Communist Party Historians' Group' (chapter 8 of this collection), and E J Hobsbawm, 'The Historians' Group of the Communist Party', in M Cornforth (ed), *Rebels and Their Causes* (London, 1978).
4 P Novick, *That Noble Dream* (Cambridge, 1988), p417; see generally ibid, ch13.
5 See E P Thompson, 'The Nehru Tradition', in E P Thompson, *Writing by Candlelight* (London, 1980), and S Sarkar, 'The Relevance of E P Thompson', in S Sarkar, *Writing Social History* (Delhi, 1997). Sarkar's *Modern India 1885-1947* (Madras, 1983) is a pioneering work of Indian history from below.
6 See A Callinicos, 'Bourgeois Revolutions and Historical Materialism', in *Marxism and the Great French Revolution* (London, 1993), pp117-118.
7 J C D Clark, *English History 1688-1832* (Cambridge, 1985), p ix.
8 F Furet, *Penser la Révolution Française* (Paris, 1978).
9 K Thomas, 'But What Does It All Mean?', *The Guardian*, 30 January 1997.
10 P Joyce, 'History and postmodernism', *Past and Present* 133 (1991), p208
11 J Derrida, *De la Grammatologie* (Paris, 1967), p227.
12 P Joyce, 'The End of Social History?', *Social History* XX (1995), p82.
13 See A Callinicos, *Against Postmodernism* (Cambridge, 1989).

14 Defenders of textualism often seek to deny that it is possible to draw such a contrast between texts and the world by pointing out that our relationship to the world is always mediated by language—we pick out objects on the basis of the classifications found in our language, and seek to characterise them in terms that, once again, derive from the language we use. This is undeniable: it is trivially true that we can only talk about things by using language. It does not follow, however, that these things are themselves constituted by language. First, we gain information about the world by physically interacting with it, even if that information is articulated linguistically. Second, discourse is not, as textualists claim, an autonomous process, but rather a social practice integrated with all the other practices through which human beings interact with the world. Thirdly, we do not simply uncritically accept linguistic representations of the world, but often subject them to scrutiny in order to select the one that seems most accurate. Historians, for example, critically examine the documents which are usually their main source of evidence in order to reconstruct the event, episode, or process they are studying. If there really were nothing outside the text this would be a pointless activity.

15 P Joyce, *Visions of the People* (Cambridge, 1991), pp11, 16.

16 Ibid, p280 (emphasis added).

17 Ibid, p339.

18 More recently Joyce, who is generally confused and eclectic in his discussion of theoretical issues, has played down textualism, instead championing what he calls 'contemporary anti-positivism'. Thus in 'The End of Social History?' he invokes the support of Michel Foucault and Anthony Giddens. It is hard to see how a coherent position can be constructed by combining the ideas of these two theorists. Foucault was famously an anti-humanist whose best-known work treated individual subjects as the effects of relations of power. Giddens is hostile to Foucault for precisely this reason: his own theory of structuration is intended to explain how human beings play an active role in the constitution and reproduction of societies: see, for example, A. Giddens, 'From Marx to Nietzsche?', in *Profiles and Critiques in Social Theory* (London, 1982). Joyce likes Giddens' theory of structuration ('End', pp89-90), but does not seem to understand that it is inconsistent with any but the most watered down version of Foucault.

19 L Wittgenstein, *On Certainty* (Oxford, 1969), section 467, p61e.

20 F Braudel, *The Mediterranean and the Mediterranean World in the Age of Philip II* (London, 1975), vol 1, p21.

21 G Arrighi, *The Long 20th Century* (London, 1994), p6-7 and passim.

22 J -F Lyotard, *The Postmodern Condition* (Manchester, 1984), p60.

23 Ibid, p82.

24 G Pandey, 'In Defence of the Fragment', *Economic and Political Weekly*, XXVI:11 and 12, 1991, p571. (The 19th century Whig Macaulay epitomised the British ruling class's disdain for Indian traditions and culture.) For a critique of this kind of thinking see S Sarker, 'The Decline of the Subaltern in Subaltern Studies', in S Sarkar, *Writing Social History*, op cit.

25 A Callinicos, *Making History* (Cambridge, 1987), pp157-72, and *Theories and Narratives* (Cambridge, 1995), pp110-128.

26 C Ginzburg, 'Microhistory: Two or Three Things That I Know About It', *Critical Inquiry* 20 (1993), pp32-33.

27 C Van Onselen, *The Seed Is Mine* (Oxford, 1996), pp7-8.

28 E Said, *Culture and Imperialism* (London, 1993), p4.

29 F Jameson, *The Political Unconscious* (London, 1981), p9.

30 It was Georg Lukács who most rigorously identified the Marxist method with the concept of totality in *History and Class Consciousness* (London, 1971): for the strengths of, but also the pitfalls involved in this approach, see J Rees, *The Algebra of Revolution* (London, 1998), ch5.

31 E P Thompson, *The Poverty of Theory and Other Essays* (London, 1978), p238.

32 E P Thompson, *The Making of the English Working Class* (London, 1980), p14.

33 Perry Anderson's *Arguments Within English Marxism* (London, 1980) remains the most thorough examination of these difficulties. See also Sam Ashman's discussion of Thompson's conception of class elsewhere in this collection.

34 L Colley, *Britons* (London, 1992), p312

35 E P Thompson, 'Which Britons?', in E P Thompson, *Persons and Polemics* (London, 1994), p328.

36 B D Palmer, *Descent into Discourse* (Philadelphia, 1990), pp138-139.

37 P Joyce, *Visions*, op cit, p14.

38 G E M de Ste Croix, *The Class Struggle in the Ancient Greek World* (London, 1981), pp43-44, 57.

39 I am well aware that the claims made in this paragraph are a promissory note rather than anything like a sustained attempt to demonstrate what is asserted, but see for further discussion my *Making History*, chs 3-5.

40 G Eley and K Nield, 'Starting Over: the Present, the Postmodern and the Moment of Social History', *Social History* XX (1995), p363. Eley and Nield appeal for support to Fredric Jameson's attempt to reconcile Marxism and postmodernism (p360): see F Jameson, *Postmodernism, or, the Cultural Logic of Late Capitalism* (London, 1991), and, for a critique of this strategy, A Callinicos, 'Drawing the Line', *International Socialism* 53 (1991).

CHAPTER 3

1 See O Hufton, *The Prospect Before Her* (London, 1995), p1.

2 S Rowbotham, *Hidden from History* (London, 1973).

3 J Liddington and J Norris, *One Hand Tied Behind Us* (London, 1978) and J Liddington, *The Life and Times of a Respectable Rebel* (London, 1984).

4 J Mitchell, *Psychoanalysis and Feminism* (London, 1975), p412.

5 H Hartmann, 'The Unhappy Marriage of Marxism and Feminism', in *Capital and Class*, no 8 (London), Summer 1979.

6 Ibid, p11.

7 I Pinchbeck, *Women and the Industrial Revolution*, p244.

8 Ibid, p244.

9 J Humphries, 'Protective Legislation, the Capitalist State and Working Class Men: the Case of the 1842 Mines Regulation Act', in *Feminist Review* (London), no 7, Spring 1981, p7.

10 C Black, *Married Women's Work* (London, 1983); R Burr Litchfield, 'The Family and the Mill', in A Wohl (ed), *The Victorian Family* (London, 1978), p182.

11 J Humphries, 'Women and Paid Work', in J Purvis (ed), *Women's History* (London, 1997), p96. Figures are based on E Higgs, 'Women's Occupations and Work in the 19th Century Censuses', in *History Workshop* 23, 1987.

12 See J Humphries, op cit, p91.

13 Ibid, p99.

14 Ibid, p100.
15 D Thompson, 'Women and 19th Century Radical Politics', in J Mitchell and A Oakley (ed), *The Rights and Wrongs of Women* (London, 1976), pp136-138.
16 Frederick Engels' letter to Karl Kautsky, 12 September 1882 in K Marx and F Engels, *Selected Correspondence* (Moscow, 1982), p330.
17 S Rowbotham, *Woman's Consciousness, Man's World* (London, 1973), p xvi.
18 For examples of this approach, see S Jeffreys, *The Spinster and her Enemies* (Melbourne, 1997) and D Spender (ed), *Feminist Theorists* (London, 1983).
19 Ibid, p62.
20 D Gittins, *Fair Sex* (London, 1982).
21 A Hacker, 'The War over the Family', *New York Review of Books*, 4 December 1997, pp34-38.

CHAPTER 4

1 F Furet, *Interpreting the French Revolution* (Cambridge, 1981).
2 For a summary of the social history school's approach see E Acton, *Rethinking the Russian Revolution* (London, 1990). For examples of the leading historians themselves see D Kaiser (ed), *The Workers' Revolution in Russia: The View From Below* (Cambridge, 1987).
3 L Schapiro, *1917: The Russian Revolutions and the Origins of Present Day Communism* (London, 1984), p219.
4 For a critique of Fitzpatrick's views in the 1970s and 1980s see G Eley, 'History with the Politics Left Out—Again?', *Russian Review*, vol 45 no 4, October 1986, pp385-394.
5 L Trotsky, *The Revolution Betrayed: What is the Soviet Union and Where is it Going?* (New York, 1972); T Cliff, *State Capitalism in Russia* (London, 1974).
6 For this argument see P Bellis, *Marxism and the USSR: the Theory of Proletarian Dictatorship and the Marxist Analysis of Soviet Society* (London, 1979).
7 S Cohen, 'Bolshevism and Stalinism' in R C Tucker (ed), *Stalinism: Essays in Historical Interpretation* (New York, 1977), pp3-29.
8 R W Davies, *Soviet History in the Gorbachev Revolution* (London, 1989), pp195-196; 'The Soviet Union in Perspective' in R W Davies (ed), *The Soviet Union* (2nd ed, London, 1989), p209.
9 D Koenker, *Moscow Workers and the 1917 Revolution* (Princeton, 1981), p364.
10 It was in order to throw some light in this dim presence in the history of the revolution that my own attempt to analyse 1917 specifically took up this issue, see M Haynes, 'Was there a Parliamentary Alternative in Russia in 1917?', *International Socialism* 76, Autumn 1997, pp3-66.
11 J Reed, *Ten Days That Shook the World* (Harmondsworth, 1966), p40.
12 See M Haynes, op cit. See also the valuable critique of the 'social history school' on this point by J E Marot, 'Class Conflict, Political Competition and Social Transformation: Critical Perspectives on the Social History of the Russian Revolution', *Revolutionary Russia*, December 1994.
13 M Malia, *The Soviet Tragedy. A History of Socialism in Russia, 1917-1991* (New York, 1994); R Pipes, *The Russian Revolution, 1899-1919* (London, 1995); *Russia Under the Bolshevik Regime, 1919-1924* (London, 1995). For critiques see P Kenez, 'The Prosecution of Soviet History: a Critique of Richard Pipes' "The Russian Revolution" ', *The Russian Review*, vol 50 no 3, July 1991, pp345-351; P Kenez, 'The Prosecution of Soviet

History volume 2', *The Russian Review*, vol 54 no 2, April 1995, pp265-269; S Smith, 'Review Essay: Richard Pipes' "The Russian Revolution" (1991)', *Social History*, vol 17 no 1, May 1992, pp329-336; I Getzler, 'Richard Pipes's "Revisionist" History of the Russian Revolution', *Slavonic and East European Review*, vol 70 no 1, January 1992, pp111-126.

14 D K Rowney, 'Russian Social History: a New Lease of Life', *Journal of Interdisciplinary History*, vol xxvi no 2, Autumn 1995, pp253-254.

15 D Volkogonov, *Stalin: Triumph and Tragedy* (London, 1991; *Trotsky: The Eternal Revolutionary* (London, 1996); *Lenin: Life and Legacy* (London, 1994). The order of translation was different from the order of writing and publication in Russia. For a critique of Volkogonov's *Lenin* see P N Siegel, 'General Volkogonov's Biography of Lenin', *Science and Society*, vol 59 no 3, Fall 1995, pp402-417.

16 R Service, *The Bolshevik Party in Revolution. A Study in Organisational Change* (London, 1979); J Rees, R Service, S Farber and R Blackburn, *In Defence of October. A Debate on the Russian Revolution* (London, 1997).

17 R Suny, 'Towards a Social History of the October Revolution', *American Historical Review*, vol 88 no 1, 1983; R G Suny, 'Revisionism and Retreat in the History of 1917: Social History and its Critics', *The Russian Review*, vol 53 no 2, April 1994, pp165-182.

18 S Smith, 'Writing the History of the Russian Revolution After the Fall of Communism', *Europe-Asia Studies*, vol 46 no 4, 1994, pp563-578. It is indicative of the state of discussion that the editors hoped that Smith's article would start a debate. It did not.

19 N Harding, *Lenin's Political Thought*, vol 1 *Theory and Practice of the Democratic Revolution* (London, 1977); N Harding, *Lenin's Political Thought*, vol 2 *Theory and Practice in the Socialist Revolution* (London, 1981); N Harding, *Leninism* (Basingstoke, 1996).

20 O Figes, *A People's Tragedy. The Russian Revolution 1891-1924* (London, 1996). When Figes' work was published it was lauded with praise by often ill-informed reviewers. Subsequently it has been treated much more harshly, see, for example, J D White, *Europe-Asia Studies*, vol 49 no 7, 1997, pp1321-1323.

21 *Lenin: The Secret Files* (Producer W Cran) Invision Films for BBC *Timewatch*, 1997.

22 R Pipes (ed), *The Unknown Lenin: From the Secret Archives* (New Haven, 1996).

23 R W Davies, 'Forced Labour under Stalin: The Archive Revelations', *New Left Review* 214, November-December 1995, pp62-86.

24 J Burbank, 'Controversies over Stalinism: Searching for a Soviet Society', *Politics and Society*, vol 19 no 3, 1991, pp325-340.

25 M Lewin, *The Gorbachev Phenomenon. A Historical Interpretation* (London, 1988), p3.

26 D Volkogonov, *Lenin* etc, op cit.

27 It is sometimes difficult not to be reminded of Orwell's story of the horror with which he learned, as a child, that 'the working class smell'. One leading Russian feminist, prominent in the West and who had better therefore remain nameless, once said to me, 'Never again should we allow ourselves to be ruled by the lumpens.'

28 *Moskovsky Komsomolets*, 19 April 1995, I am indebted to Dave Crouch for this reference.

29 A Yakolev, *The Fate of Marxism in Russia* (New Haven, 1993).

30 A Nove, *An Economic History of the USSR* (Harmondsworth, 1992), p207.

31 For some basic data on the shift in the ruling class (described as a shift in

elite power) see O Krshtanovskaya and S White, 'From Soviet Nomenklatura to Russian Elite', *Europe-Asia Studies*, vol 48 no 6, 1966, pp711-733.

32 For a short summary of the argument on the 1920s and for two contrasting interpretations which see a degeneration towards state capitalism see M Haynes, *Nikolai Bukharin and the Transition from Capitalism to Socialism* (London, 1985) and D Gluckstein, *The Tragedy of Bukharin* (London, 1992).

33 Peter Sedgwick's introduction to V Serge, *Year One of the Russian Revolution* (London, 1972).

34 The data for 1920 comes from D Koenker, 'Urbanisation and De-urbanistion in the Russian Revolution and Civil War', *Journal of Modern History*, vol 57, September 1985, p425, who relies on the census of that year. For the earlier figures I have preferred the data from A Rashin, *Naselenie Rossii za 100 let, 1811-1913gg, Statisticheskie Ocherki* (Moscow, 1956) to that presented by Koenker who mysteriously ignores this standard source.

35 Quoted L Lih, 'Bolshevik Razvertska and War Communism', *Slavic Review*, vol 45 no 4, Winter 1986, pp678-679.

36 K D Patterson, 'Typhus and its Control in Russia 1870-1940', *Medical History*, vol 37, 1993, pp361-381.

37 E G Gimpelíson, *Sovetskii rabochii klass 1918-1920gg. Sotsialíno-politicheskie izmeneniya* (Moscow, 1974), pp77-78. Readers might be perplexed by different figures that exist for the number of workers. Contemporary, and subsequent, accounts focused on factory workers and miners. The working class as a whole was of course much wider than these two groups. Indeed they made up a minority of the working class as a whole, albeit still the central core. Data for this core was then collected in different ways and is sometimes presented as an annual average and sometimes for a particular date. With the very rapid decline in numbers in the civil war there is obviously a significant difference between start and end years figures and the annual average data.

38 A V Gogolevskii, *Petrogradskii sovet v godui grazdanskoi voinui* (Leningrad, 1987), pp56-70.

39 Quoted in O Anweiller, *The Soviets: The Russian Workers, Peasants and Soldiers Councils, 1905-1921* (New York, 1974), p232.

40 Quoted in I Deutscher, *The Prophet Armed: Trotsky 1879-1921* (London, 1954), p90.

41 R Service, op cit.

42 A V Gogolevskii, op cit, pp191-192.

43 V Serge, *Revolution in Danger: Writings from Russia 1919-1921* (London, 1997).

44 L T Lih, 'The Mystery of the ABC', *Slavic Review*, vol 56 no 1, Spring 1997, pp50-72.

45 Quoted in K D Patterson, op cit.

46 *Bulletin de la Ligue de la Régénération de la Russie* as reprinted in *The Russian Commonwealth*, vol1 no 3, 1 Dec 1918, p79.

47 H Kukk, 'The Failure of Yudenich's North-western Army in 1919: A Dissenting White Russian View', *Journal of Baltic Studies*, vol xii no 4, 1981, pp362-383.

48 R Pipes, 'Black Bread', *The New Republic*, 31 March 1997, pp36-40.

49 *The Times*, 11 August 1921.

50 'The Famine: Report by Kalinin May 12', *Russian Information and Review*, vol 1 no 18, 15 June 1922, p413.

CHAPTER 5

I am grateful for helpful comments on an earlier draft of this essay from Norah Carlin and John Rees.

1   K Marx and F Engels, *Selected Works* (2 vols, Moscow, 1950), vol 1, pp28, 33, 50.
2   K Kautsky, *The Materialist Conception of History* (New Haven, 1988), pp252, 254.
3   K Marx, *Capital*, vol 1 (Everyman Library, 1930), pp235-237.
4   M Dobb, 'From Feudalism to Capitalism', in R H Hilton (ed), *The Transition from Feudalism to Capitalism* (London, 1976), pp165-167; F Engels, *Socialism: Utopian and Scientific* (London, 1993), pp89, 110-111.
5   B Porchnev, 'Popular Uprisings in France before the Fronde, 1623-1648', in P J Coveney (ed), *France in Crisis 1620-1657* (London, 1977), p91.
6   L Stone, 'Social Mobility in England, 1500-1700', *Past and Present*, no 33 (1966), p17.
7   N Carlin, 'Marxism and the English Civil War', *International Socialism* 10 (1980-81), pp114-115.
8   F Engels, op cit, p59.
9   S Rappaport, *Worlds Within Worlds: Structures of Life in 16th Century London* (Cambridge, 1989), pp238-284, 326-376.
10 N Carlin, 'Liberty and Fraternities in the English Revolution: The Politics of London Artisans' Protests, 1635-1659', *International Review of Social History*, no 39 (1994), pp249-251; E Kerridge, *Textile Manufactures in Early Modern England* (Manchester, 1985), pp193, 201, 213.
11 *The Apprentices of London's Petition* (London, 1641); W L Sachse (ed), *The Diurnal of Thomas Rugg, 1659-1661*, Camden Society, 3rd series, vol XCI (1961), p9; M James, *Social Problems and Policy during the Puritan Revolution* (London, 1930), pp210-212.
12 T Harris, *London Crowds in the Reign of Charles II* (Cambridge, 1987), pp191-192.
13 A Everitt, 'Farm Labourers', in Joan Thirsk (ed), *The Agrarian History of England and Wales*, vol IV (Cambridge, 1967), pp398-399.
14 B Sharp, *In Contempt of All Authority: Rural Artisans and Riot in the West of England, 1586-1660* (Berkeley, 1980), pp156-174, 257-260.
15 R H Tawney, 'The Assessment of Wages in England by the Justices of the Peace', in W E Minchinton (ed), *Wage Regulation in Pre-Industrial England* (Newton Abbot, 1972), pp63, 65.
16 A Everitt, op cit, pp398-400; D Woodward, 'Wage Rates and Living Standards in Pre-Industrial England', *Past and Present*, no 91 (1981), pp39-42, 44-45; A L Beier, *Masterless Men: the Vagrancy Problem in England, 1560-1640* (London, 1985), p26.
17 D Woodward, op cit, pp44-45; E Kerridge, op cit, pp176-178, 187-192; J M Neeson, *Commoners: Common Right, Enclosure and Social Change in England, 1700-1820* (Cambridge, 1996), pp297-319.
18 Q Hoare and G Nowell-Smith (eds), *Selections from the Prison Notebooks of Antonio Gramsci* (London, 1971), p75; T Shanin (ed), *Peasants and Peasant Societies* (Harmondsworth, 1971), pp15-16.
19 V I Lenin, 'Preliminary Draft of Theses on the Agrarian Question', in V I Lenin, *Selected Works* (2 vols, London, 1947), vol 2, pp645-646.
20 C Lis and H Soly, *Poverty and Capitalism in Pre-Industrial Europe* (Atlantic Highlands, 1979), p217.
21 A Soboul, *The Parisian Sans-Culottes and the French Revolution 1793-94* (Oxford, 1964), pp51-52.

22 D Goodman and M Redclift, *From Peasant to Proletarian: Capitalist Development and Agrarian Transition* (Oxford, 1981), pp85-93, 96-98.

23 E Lipson, *The Economic History of England*, vol 2 (5th edn, London, 1948), pp xxvi-xxvii; I Wallerstein, *The Modern World System*, vol 2 (New York, 1980), p.195; M Gould, *Revolution in the Development of Capitalism: The Coming of the English Revolution* (Berkeley, 1987), pp155-156.

24 T Hobbes, *Leviathan* (Michael Oakeshott (ed), Oxford, no date), p161; T Hobbes, *Behemoth or The Long Parliament* (Ferdinand Tönnies (ed), 2nd edn, London, 1969), p126.

25 C Middleton, 'Women's Labour and the Transition to Pre-Industrial Capitalism', in L Charles and L Duffin (eds), *Women and Work in Pre-Industrial England* (London, 1985), p194; J Merrington, 'Town and Country in the Transition to Capitalism', in R H Hilton (ed), op cit, pp189-190.

26 T M Safley and L N Rosenband (eds), *The Workplace before the Factory: Artisans and Proletarians 1500-1800* (Ithaca, 1993), pp6-7, 10.

27 G V Plekhanov, *In Defence of Materialism* (London, 1947), p147.

28 K Marx, op cit, vol 1, pp379-381; F Engels, op cit, pp101, 111; R Brenner, 'Bourgeois Revolution and the Transition to Capitalism', in A L Beier, D Cannadine and J M Rosenheim (eds), *The First Modern Society* (Cambridge, 1989), pp292-294. Brenner's theorisings lack an understanding of the role of the small producers.

29 K Marx, op cit, vol 1, ch 24.

30 H Medick, 'The Transition from Feudalism to Capitalism', in R Samuel (ed), *People's History and Socialist Theory* (London, 1981), p124; J M Neeson, op cit, pp81, 106-109, 177-178, 259-293.

31 M James, op cit, pp192-223; G Unwin, *Industrial Organisation in the 16th and 17th Centuries* (reprinted London, 1957), pp197, 199, 207-208; N Carlin, 'Liberty and Fraternities in the English Revolution: The Politics of London Artisans' Protests, 1635-1659', *International Review of Social History*, no 39 (1994), pp231-235, 237-251.

32 H Medick, op cit, p124; C Lis and H Soly, op cit, pp150-151; D Goodman and M Redclift, op cit, pp24, 53-54, 62-63, 71, 95; A D Lublinskaya, *French Absolutism: The Crucial Phase, 1620-1629* (Cambridge, 1968), pp55, 68; D Parker, *Class and State in Ancien Regime France: the Road to Modernity?* (London, 1996), p237; M Gould, op cit, p165.

33 K Kautsky, op cit, pp372-373.

34 F Peck, *Desiderata Curiosa*, vol 2 (London, 1735), bk xii, pp23-25.

35 *Reliquiae Baxterianae* (Matthew Sylvester (ed), London, 1696), p94.

36 J Corbet, *An Historicall Relation of the Military Government of Gloucester* (London, 1645), p9.

37 Quoted by P Zagorin, *A History of Political Thought in the English Revolution* (reprinted Bristol, 1997), p31.

38 'More Light Shining in Buckingham-shire' (1649), in G H Sabine (ed), *The Works of Gerrard Winstanley* (New York, 1965), pp627-628, 633-634; J Lilburne, 'The Legall Fundamentall Liberties of the People of England' (1649), in W Haller and G Davies (eds), *The Leveller Tracts 1647-1653* (Gloucester, Massachusetts, 1964), p439.

39 Quoted by C Hill, *Economic Problems of the Church* (Oxford, 1956), p156.

40 K Marx, op cit, vol 1, pp844-847.

41 C B Macpherson, *The Political Theory of Possessive Individualism* (Oxford, 1962), pp148-154, 214-220; C B Macpherson, *Democratic Theory* (Oxford, 1973), pp129-133.

42 D M Wolfe (ed), *Leveller Manifestoes of the Puritan Revolution* (London, 1944), pp288, 390-391; D B Robertson, *The Religious Foundations of Leveller Democracy* (New York, 1951), p87.

43 T Johnson, *Plea for Free-mens Liberties* (1646).

44 *Englands Troublers Troubled* (1648).

45 D M Wolfe (ed), op cit, pp275-276.

46 R H Hilton, *Class Conflict and the Crisis of Feudalism* (2nd edn, London, 1990), pp83-84, 108-109; M Dobb, *Studies in the Development of Capitalism* (London, 1946), p7.

47 Quoted by G Unwin, op cit, p212.

48 M Dobb, op cit, p20.

49 K Marx, 'The Eighteenth Brumaire of Louis Bonaparte', in K Marx and F Engels, op cit, vol 1, pp302-303; G Lukács, *History and Class Consciousness* (London, 1971), pp55-62; K Kautsky, op cit, pp252-253; G Rudé, *Ideology and Popular Protest* (London, 1980), p27; R H Hilton, *The English Peasantry in the Later Middle Ages* (Oxford, 1975), Ch1.

50 K Kautsky, op cit, pp252-253, 367.

51 K Lindley, *Fenland Riots and the English Revolution* (London, 1982), ch 5; B Sharp, op cit, pp250-256.

52 R B Manning, *Village Revolts: Social Protest and Popular Disturbances in England, 1509-1640* (Oxford, 1988), pp127-129; B Sharp, 'Common Rights, Charities, and the Disorderly Poor', in G Eley and W Hunt (eds), *Reviving the English Revolution* (London, 1988), pp126-127; J Walter, 'A Rising of the People? The Oxfordshire Rising of 1596', *Past and Present*, no 107 (1985), pp120-122; J M Neeson, 'The Opponents of Enclosure in 18th Century Northamptonshire', *Past and Present*, no 105 (1984), pp138-139; S Hindle, 'Persuasion and Protest in the Cuddington Common Enclosure Dispute 1635-1639', *Past and Present*, no 158 (1998), pp69-76.

53 J Thirsk, 'Agrarian Problems in the English Revolution', in R C Richardson (ed), *Town and Countryside in the English Revolution* (Manchester, 1992).

54 D M Wolfe (ed), op cit, p270.

55 C Webster, *The Great Instauration: Science, Medicine and Reform 1626-1660* (London, 1975), pp361-362, 455-456; J O Appleby, *Economic Thought and Ideology in 17th Century England* (Princeton, 1978), ch 6; C Lis and H Soly, op cit, p127.

56 *Long Parliament Work* (London, 1659); *Chaos* (London, 1659); W Sprigge, *A Modest Plea* (London, 1659); *Englands Safety in the Laws Supremacy* (London, 1659).

57 P S Seaver, *Wellington's World: A Puritan Artisan in 19th Century London* (London, 1985), pp123-124; D Veall, *The Popular Movement for Law Reform 1640-1660* (Oxford, 1970), pp12-17, 145-151; B S Capp, *The Fifth Monarchy Men* (London, 1972), pp161-168.

58 M Ashley, *Financial and Commercial Policy under the Cromwellian Protectorate* (2nd edn, London, 1962), p175; J Thirsk (ed), *The Agrarian History of England and Wales*, vol V, pt ii (Cambridge, 1985), p879; D Hirst, 'Locating the 1650s in England's 17th Century', *History*, no 263 (1996), pp377, 379.

59 R H Tawney, op cit, pp65, 67-68.

60 P Chamberlen, *The Poore Mans Advocate* (London, 1649), p20.

61 A L Beier, 'Poverty and Progress in Early Modern England', in A L Beier, D Cannadine and J M Rosenheim (eds), op cit, p228; D C Coleman, 'Labour in the English Economy in the 17th Century', in E M Carus-Wilson (ed), *Essays in Economic History*, vol 2 (London, 1962), pp300-304; P Slack, *Poverty and Policy in Tudor and Stuart England* (London, 1988), pp65-66.

62 J Cooke, *Unum Necessarium: Or, The Poore Mans Case* (London, 1648), pp27-28, 43.

63 *Tyranipocrit* (Rotterdam, 1649), pp17, 24.

64 *Trades Destruction is Englands Ruine* (London, 1659).

65 R Coster, 'A Mite Cast into the Common Treasury', in G H Sabine (ed), op cit, pp656-657.

66 K Thomas, 'Another Digger Broadside', *Past and Present*, no 42 (1961), pp62-63.

67 G Winstanley, 'A New-Yeers Gift for the Parliament and Armie' (1650), in G H Sabine (ed), op cit, p388.

68 K Thomas, op cit; J Gurney, 'Gerrard Winstanley and the Digger Movement in Walton and Cobham', *The Historical Journal*, vol 37 (1994); S Hindle, op cit, pp76-77.

69 A Everitt, op cit, pp440-441, 464-465.

70 J A Sharp, *Crime in 17th Century England* (Cambridge, 1983), pp18-19, 204, 208-209.

71 B Sharp, *In Contempt of All Authority: Rural Artisans and Riot in the West of England, 1586-1660* (Berkeley, 1980), pp8, 264.

72 F J Fisher, 'The Growth of London', in E W Ives (ed), *The English Revolution 1600-1660* (London, 1968), p78; J Merrington, op cit, pp187-188; C Hill, *The World Turned Upside Down* (London, 1972), pp33-34, 35-36; H Burstin, 'Unskilled Labour in Paris', in T M Safley and L N Rosenband (eds), op cit, pp63-64.

73 K Marx, 'The Eighteenth Brumaire', in K Marx and F Engels, op cit, vol 1, p267.

74 A L Beier, op cit, pp42, 46.

75 C Hill, 'Pottage for Freeborn Englishmen: Attitudes to Wage Labour', in *Change and Continuity in 17th Century England* (London, 1974); C Hill, *Liberty Against the Law* (London, 1996).

76 K Kautsky, op cit, p487.

77 D McLellan (ed), *Marx's Grundrisse* (London, 1973), p69.

78 I Gentles, *The New Model Army in England, Ireland and Scotland, 1645-1653* (Oxford, 1992), pp31-40.

79 D McLellan (ed), op cit, p134.

80 A Everitt, op cit, p464.

81 *Pay Provision and Good Accommadation for the Privat Soldiers* (manuscript), British Library, E.537(8); *A Moderate and Cleer Relation of the Private Souldiers of Colonell Scroops and Col Sanders Regiments* (London, 1648); *A Friendly Letter of Advice to the Souldiers* (1659).

82 C H Firth, *Cromwell's Army* (with a new introduction by P H Hardacre, London, 1962), pp204-206.

83 *The Diurnal of Thomas Rugg*, op cit, p42.

84 *The Sentinels Remonstrance* (London, 1659).

85 J T Rutt (ed), *Diary of Thomas Burton* (4 vols, London, 1828), vol 1, p228.

86 B Sharp, op cit, p254; B Sharp, 'Rural Discontent and the English Revolution', in R C Richardson, op cit, p262; D O Pam, *The Rude Multitude: Enfield and the Civil War* (Edmonton Hundred Historical Society, 1977), Occasional Paper (New Series), no 33, p12.

87 K Marx and F Engels, *The German Ideology* (Moscow, 1976), pp68-69.

88 D Hirst, op cit, pp379-381; K Wrightson, *English Society 1580-1680* (London, 1982), pp223, 226.

89 K Marx, 'The Bourgeoisie and the Counter-Revolution', in K Marx and F Engels, op cit, vol 1, p64; F Engels, op cit, pp42, 62-63.

90 L Trotsky, *History of the Russian Revolution* (London, 1977), pp588-589.

CHAPTER 6

1 R Gray, 'Class, Politics and Historical "Revisionism"', *Social History*, vol 19, no 1, May 1994.

2 P Joyce, 'The End of Social History?', *Social History*, vol 20, no 1, January 1995, pp75-76.

3 Ibid, p83.

4 Ibid, p77

5 J Vernon, 'Who is Afraid of the Linguistic Turn?', *Social History*, vol 19, no1, January 1994, pp86-87.

6 P Joyce, 'The End of Social History?', op cit, p82.

7 P Joyce, *Visions of the People: Industrial England and the Question of Class 1848-1914* (Cambridge, 1991), pp28-29.

8 G Stedman Jones, *Languages of Class: Studies in English Working Class History 1832-1982* (Cambridge, 1987), pp102-104.

9 Ibid, p107.

10 J Vernon, 'Whose afraid of the Linguistic Turn?', op cit, pp86-87.

11 P Joyce, *Visions of the People: Industrial England and the Question of Class 1848-1914* (Cambridge, 1991), p84.

12 Ibid, p29.

13 For a good review of some of the recent literature see R Price, 'Languages of Revisionism', *Journal of Social History*, Fall 1996.

14 M Taylor, *The Decline of British Radicalism* (Oxford, 1995), p338

15 James Vernon stands out as something of an oddity, even amongst the postmodernists. For Vernon the significance of working class suffrage was that it actually represented a de-democratisation of society. In his book *Politics and the People* (Cambridge, 1993) he traces instead the radical tradition back to the rough and tumble of parish politics in which elections were rowdy and colourful affairs. They were also, of course, events in which most of the participants were not entitled to vote and in which loyalties were bought and sold with drink!

16 E F Biagini and A J Reid, 'Currents of Radicalism', in *Currents of Radicalism: Popular Radicalism, Organised Labour and Party Politics in Britain, 1850-1914* (Cambridge, 1991), p10.

17 N Kirk, 'Class and the "Linguistic Turn" in Chartist and Post-Chartist Historiography', in *Social Class and Marxism* (Scolar Press, 1996), p101.

18 Quoted by J Charlton, *The Chartists* (London, 1997), p37.

19 T B Macaulay, *History of England*, vol 1, ch 2.

20 Quoted by N Kirk in *The Growth of Working Class Reformism in Mid-Victorian England* (Croom Helm, 1985), p88.

21 J Vincent, *Pollbooks: How Victorians Voted* (Cambridge, 1967), p59.

22 Engels quoted by N Kirk, op cit, p87.

23 E J Hobsbawm, 'Trends in the British Labour Movement since 1850', in *Labouring Men: Studies in the History of Labour* (Weidenfeld & Nicholson, 1964), p323.

24 N Kirk, op cit, p89.

25 Ibid, p98.

26 For a quick summary of the most important statistics on the expansion of industry after 1850 see the discussion by Humphry Southall, drawing on Raphael Samuel's study, in *An Atlas of Industrial Protest in Britain 1750-1990* (Macmillan, 1996), pp59-64.

27 G Stedman Jones, 'Class Struggle and the Industrial Revolution', *New Left Review* 90, 1975.

28 P Joyce, *Work, Society and Politics: The Culture of the Factory in Later Victorian England* (Brighton, 1980).

29 See the account of this given in 'The Roots of Reformism', in T Rothstein, *From Chartism to Labourism* (Martin Lawrence, 1929).

30 G Dangerfield, *The Strange Death of Liberal England* (Serif, 1997), p195.

31 For a useful discussion of the 'Labour Aristocracy' see K Corr and A Brown, 'The Labour Aristocracy and the Roots of Reformism', *International Socialism* 59, 1993.

32 C Hill, *A Nation of Change and Novelty* (London, 1993), ch 3.

33 R Groves, *We Shall Rise Again: A Narrative History of Chartism* (Secker and Warburg, 1938).

34 For a classic discussion of this see, 'The Historian and His Facts', in E H Carr, *What is History?* (Penguin, 1961).

35 F Engels, *The Peasant Wars in Germany*, in K Marx and F Engels, *Basic Writings on Politics and Philosophy* (Anchor Books, 1959), pp414-415.

36 K Marx, *The Eighteenth Brumaire of Louis Bonaparte*, in K Marx and F Engels, *Basic Writings on Politics and Philosophy* (Anchor Books, 1950), p320.

37 A Briggs, 'The Language of "Class" in Early 19th Century England', in R S Neale (ed), *History and Class* (Blackwells, 1983), p29.

CHAPTER 7

1 P Anderson, 'Origins of the Present Crisis', in P Anderson and R Blackburn (eds), *Towards Socialism* (Fontana, 1965), p21.

2 Ibid, p25.

3 Ibid, p25.

4 G Stedman Jones, *Outcast London* (Pantheon, 1984), p xiv.

5 Ibid, p xiv.

6 K Marx and F Engels, *The German Ideology* (Progress, 1976), p220.

7 K Marx and F Engels, *Marx and Engels on Britain* (Progress, 1971), p345.

8 Figures from R Samuel, 'The Workshop of the World', *History Workshop*, no 3, 1977, pp6-72.

9 C H Lee, 'Regional Growth and Structural Change in Victorian Britain', *Economic History Review*, 2nd series, xxiv, 1981, pp438-452.

10 E P Thompson, *Persons and Polemics* (Merlin, 1994), p27.

11 G Stedman Jones, op cit, p343.

12 Y Kapp, *Eleanor Marx: Family Life 1855-1883* (Virago, 1979), p73.

13 H Collins and C Abramsky, *Karl Marx and the British Labour Movement* (Macmillan, 1965), p21.

14 J McPherson, *Drawn With the Sword* (Oxford University Press, 1996), p226.

15 H Collins and C Abramsky, op cit, p14.

16 Y Kapp, *Eleanor Marx: Family Life 1855-1883* (Virago, 1979), p73.

17 K Marx and F Engels, *Ireland and the Irish Question* (Progress, 1978), p161.

18 K Marx and F Engels, *Marx and Engels on Britain*, op cit, pp355-356.

CHAPTER 8

1 Quoted in B D Palmer, *E P Thompson: Objections and Oppositions* (London, 1994), pp50-51.

2 Quoted in H J Kaye, *The British Marxist Historians* (New York, 1995), pp133-134.

3 E J Hobsbawm, 'The Historians' Group of the Communist Party', in M Cornforth (ed), *Rebels and Their Causes* (London, 1978), p25.

4   See D Parker, 'The Communist Party Historians' Group', *Socialist History*
    12 (London, 1997), p41.
5   E J Hobsbawm, op cit, p26.
6   Ibid, p29.
7   D Parker, op cit, p47.
8   E J Hobsbawm, op cit, p23.
9   Interview with Christopher Hill, *International Socialism* 56, Autumn 1992,
    p128.
10 E P Thompson, *The Making of the English Working Class*, (London,
    1988), p12.
11 Ibid, pp8-11.
12 Quoted in A Callinicos, *The Revolutionary Ideas of Karl Marx* (London,
    1983), p142.
13 Ibid, p99.
14 P Anderson, *Arguments Within English Marxism* (London, 1980), p43.
15 E P Thompson, *Whigs and Hunters* (Harmondsworth, 1977), pp267-268.
16 Ibid, p267.
17 See, for example, 'Trial by Jury', in *Writing by Candlelight* (London,
    1980), p230.
18 E P Thompson, 'The Poverty of Theory', in *The Poverty of Theory and
    Other Essays* (London, 1978), p164.
19 Quoted in D Parker, op cit, p42.
20 C Hill, 'The Norman Yoke', in *Puritanism and Revolution: Studies in
    Interpretation of the English Revolution of the 17th Century* (London,
    1958), pp46-112.
21 E J Hobsbawm, op cit, p44.
22 E J Hobsbawm, *The Age of Empire 1875-1914*, (London, 1994), p131.
23 Ibid, p129.
24 *The Sunday Times*, 27 April 1975, quoted in P Anderson, op cit, p193.
25 E P Thompson, 'An Open Letter to Leszek Kolakowski' in *The Poverty of
    Theory*, op cit, pp313-314.
26 Ibid, p319.
27 See the interview with Hill, op cit.
28 C Hill, *The Experience of Defeat: Milton and Some Contemporaries*
    (London, 1994), p322.

CHAPTER 9

1   F Engels, *Principles of Communism* (Peking, 1977), p1.
2   M Shaw, *Marxism and Social Science, the Roots of Social Knowledge*
    (Pluto Press, 1975), p83.
3   L Stone, *The Past and Present Revisited* (Routledge and Kegan Paul,
    1987), pp5-6.
4   Ibid, pp6-7.
5   Quoted in J McPherson, 'What's the Matter with History?' in *Drawn with
    the Sword, Reflections on the American Civil War* (Oxford, 1996),
    p237.
6   M Shaw, op cit, p53.
7   L Stone, op cit, p7.
8   P Kennedy, *The Rise and Fall of the Great Powers* (Fontana, 1989) and
    Preparing for the Twenty-First Century (Harper Collins, 1993).
9   For Marx and Engels' case against Dühring, see Engels', *Anti-Dühring*. For a
    Marxist reply to Anthony Giddens see A Callinicos, 'Anthony Giddens: A
    Contemporary Critique' in A Callinicos (ed), *Marxist Theory* (OUP, 1989).

See also the debate between Anthony Giddens and John Rees in *Socialist Review*, no 210, July-August 1997.

10 See E Rickword, 'Milton: the Revolutionary Intellectual' in C Hill (ed), *The English Revolution 1640* (Lawrence & Wishart, 1940), p112. This edition contains three essays wheras subsequent editions only contain Christopher Hill's essay, from which the original collection took its title.

11 For a modern defence of the Marxist analysis of the French Revolution and a critique of revisionism see P McGarr and A Callinicos, *Marxism and the Great French Revolution* (International Socialism, 1993); for the English Revolution see J Rees, 'Revolution Denied' in L German and R Hoveman (eds), *A Socialist Review* (Bookmarks, 1997); for the Russian Revolution see J Rees et al, *In Defence of October, a Debate on the Russian Revolution* (Bookmarks, 1997).

12 L Stone, op cit, p15.

13 See R Grassby, 'The Decline of Falconry in Early Modern England', *Past and Present*, no 157, November 1997.

14 L Stone, op cit, p42.

15 P Anderson, *Considerations on Western Marxism* (Verso, 1979), p29. Anderson is right to see Western Europe as the point of departure for this tradition, but it quickly spread, especially to America. Moreover, it eventually became universal. This is why it is preferable to describe it as academic Marxism, since its root and soil are social not geographic. For Anderson's further reflections on, and retreat from, some of the positions outlined in *Considerations on Western Marxism*, see P Anderson, *In the Tracks of Historical Materialism* (Verso, 1983).

16 M Shaw, op cit, p102.

17 V I Lenin, *Collected Works*, vol 1 (Moscow, 1966), pp400-401.

Further reading

Classics

The following works by Marx and Engels are a good place to start:

The German Ideology (student edition, edited by Chris Arthur).

The Holy Family (K Marx and F Engels, *Collected Works*, vol 4).

Introduction to the *Grundisse*.

Preface and Introduction to *Contribution to a Critique of Political Economy*.

Other useful reading

Chris Harman, *Marxism and History*.

Georg Lukács, *History and Class Consciousness*.

Alex Callinicos and Paul McGarr, *Marxism and the Great French Revolution*.

John Rees, 'Revolution Denied' and 'National Peculiarity in British History', in L German and R Hoveman (eds), *A Socialist Review*.

Alex Callinicos, *Against Postmodernism*.

E H Carr, *What is History?*

Geoffrey De Ste Croix, *Class Struggle in the Ancient Greek World*.

Franz Jakubowski, *Ideology and Superstructure in Historical Materialism*.

Antonio Labriola, *Essays in the Materialist Conception of History*.

Harvey Kaye, *The British Marxist Historians*.

Richard Evans, *In Defence of History*.

Contributors

Chris Harman is editor of *Socialist Worker* and author of *Economics of the Madhouse, Explaining the Crisis, How Marxism Works* and *The Lost revolution: Germany 1918 to 1923*.

Alex Callinicos is professor of politics at York University and author of *Is there a Future for Marxism?*, *Marxism and Philosophy, The Revolutionary Ideas of Karl Marx, Against Postmodernism, Making History, The Revenge of History* and *Theories and Narratives*.

Lindsey German is editor of *Socialist Review* and author of *Sex, Class and Socialism* and *A Question of Class*.

Mike Haynes is senior lecturer in European studies at the University of Wolverhampton and author of *Nikolai Bukharin: and the Transition from Capitalism to Socialism* and many articles on the history of Eastern Europe and the Russian Revolution.

Brian Manning is emeritus professor of history at the University of Ulster and author of *The English People and the English Revolution, 1649: The Crisis of the English Revolution* and *Aristocrats, Plebeians and Revolution in England*.

Mark O'Brien lectures at Tower Hamlets College, London and is author of *'Perish the Privileged Orders': a Socialist History of the Chartist Movement*.

Chris Bambery is a national organiser for the Socialist Workers Party and author of *Ireland's Permanent Revolution*.

Sam Ashman is a journalist with *Socialist Worker*.

John Rees is editor of *International Socialism* and the author of *The ABC of Socialism, In Defence of October* and *The Algebra of Revolution: The Dialectic and the Classical Marxist Tradition*.

Index